OUR AWESOME GOD

OUR AWESOME GOD

John MacArthur

CROSSWAY BOOKS • WHEATON, ILLINOIS
A DIVISION OF GOOD NEWS PUBLISHERS

Library of Congress Cataloging-in-Publication Data
MacArthur, John, 1939-
   [God]
   Our awesome God / John Mac Arthur.
     p.   cm.
   Originaly published: Wheaton, Ill. : Victor Books, c1993, in series:
MacArthur study series.
   ISBN 1-58134-289-6 (pbk. : alk. paper)
   1. God. 2. God—Biblical teaching. I. Title.
BT103 .M23   2001
231—dc21   2001003417
                                    CIP

15	14	13	12	11	10	09	08	07	06	05	04	03	02	01
15	14	13	12	11	10	9	8	7	6	5	4	3	2	

CONTENTS

INTRODUCTION

There is an old fable about six men blind from birth who lived in India. One day they decided to visit a nearby palace. When they arrived, an elephant was standing in the courtyard. The first blind man touched the side of the elephant and said, "An elephant is like a wall." The second blind man touched the trunk and said, "An elephant is like a snake." The third blind man touched the tusk and said, "An elephant is like a spear." The fourth blind man touched the leg and said, "An elephant is like a tree." The fifth blind man touched the ear and said, "An elephant is like a fan." The sixth blind man touched the tail and said, "An elephant is like a rope." Because each blind man touched only one part of the elephant, none of them could agree on what an elephant is really like.

Bringing that analogy into the spiritual realm, many people have misconceptions about what God is really like. Believing the wrong thing about God is a serious matter because it is idolatry. Does that surprise you? Contrary to popular belief, idolatry is more than bowing down to a small figure or worshiping in a pagan temple. According to the Bible, it is thinking anything about God that isn't true or attempting to transform Him into something He isn't.

God Himself pointed out the fallacy of idolatry, saying of man, "You thought that I was just like you" (Ps. 50:21). We must be careful not to think of God in our terms or entertain thoughts that are unworthy of Him. It is perilously easy to do both.

Voltaire, the French agnostic, once quipped that God created man in His own image, and man returned the favor. "Not only is that true of ungodly men," writes one author, "but Christians are often guilty of the error as well. Because we are finite beings, we tend to perceive the infinite in light of our own limitations. Even Scripture itself presents truth in language and thoughts that accommodate our human understanding. But even though it speaks down to us, the Bible also encourages us to reach beyond our limitations and think exalted thoughts about God. It is essential that our ideas of God correspond as nearly as possible to what He really is like. Instead we often put God in a box— and our box is incredibly small! We tend to let our culture instead of our Creator determine what we value. Those values influence our thoughts about God and shape the way we relate to Him in our daily experience" (Gregg Cantelmo, "Criminal Concepts of God," *Masterpiece* magazine [September/October 1989], p. 5).

The only way to know what God is like is to discover what He has revealed about Himself in Scripture. The revelation of God's nature falls into different categories of attributes, which in their totality define His character.

What does Scripture say about God? To begin with, in the fullest sense He is incomprehensible. Zophar got that one fact right in his misdirected rebuke against Job: "Can you discover the depths of God? Can you discover the limits of the Almighty? They are as high as the heavens, what can you do? Deeper than Sheol, what can you know? Its measure is longer than the earth and broader than the sea. If He passes by or shuts up, or calls an assembly, who can restrain Him?" (Job 11:7-10). David said it this way: "Great is the LORD, and highly to be praised; and His greatness is unsearchable" (Ps. 145:3). God is infinite—there is no end to Him.

To define the infinite God in ways we can understand, we often have to state what He is not for a basis of comparison. For example, when we say that God is holy, we mean He has no sin. We cannot conceive of absolute holiness since we're all too familiar with sin. As we study about God in the following chapters, we will often take that comparative approach so we can gain a fuller understanding of His key attributes.

Knowing what God is like is foundational to knowing God Himself. And knowing God is the essence of being a Christian. The apostle John wrote, "This is eternal life, *that they may know You*, the only true God, and Jesus Christ whom You have sent" (John 17:3, emphasis added). When most people hear the term *eternal life*, they think of life that goes on forever. But Scripture affirms that, more than that, eternal life is a quality of life for the person who knows God.

Tragically, many Christians today have set their affections on the temporal things of this world, exchanging their great privilege of knowing God better for that which is mundane. God Himself rebukes that kind of thinking, for He declared, "Let not a wise man boast of his wisdom, and let not the mighty man boast of his might, let not a rich man boast of his riches; but let him who boasts boast of this, that he understands and knows Me" (Jer. 9:23-24).

What does the Lord delight in? Not our boasting of worldly wisdom, human prowess, or material gain. He delights that we know Him. In his book *A Heart for God*, Sinclair Ferguson probes further:

> What do you and I boast about? What subject of conversation most arouses us and fills our hearts? Do we consider knowing God to be the greatest treasure in the world, and by far our greatest privilege? If not, we are but pygmies in the world of the Spirit. We have sold our Christian birthright for a mess of pottage, and our true Christian experience will be superficial, inadequate, and tragically out of focus. ([Carlisle, Penn.: The Banner of Truth Trust, 1987], p. 4)

Rather than sell our spiritual birthright, we must learn to say with David, "O God, You are my God; I shall seek You earnestly; my soul thirsts for You, my flesh yearns for You . . . to see Your power and Your glory" (Ps. 63:1-2).

Although this book is not an exhaustive study on the character of God, I trust it will help you to know what God is like and will serve as an incentive to know Him better. Read the following pages prayerfully. Scripture promises that you will find God "if you search for Him with all your heart and all your soul" (Deut. 4:29). Learn to say with the apostle Paul, "My determined purpose is that I may know Him—that I may progressively become more deeply and intimately acquainted with Him, perceiving and recognizing and understanding the wonders of His person more strongly and more clearly" (Phil. 3:10, AMP).

1

OUR TRIUNE GOD

Who is God? In his book *The Future of an Illusion,* Sigmund Freud, the father of psychoanalysis, said God is an invention of man (New York: W.W. Norton, 1961). We desperately need security, he wrote, because we have deep-seated fears of living in a threatening world in which we have little control over our circumstances. Freud claimed that we invent God as a protective father, and he suggested three reasons for our doing so.

His first reason is that we fear nature—we fear its unpredictability, impersonality, and ruthlessness. Because we all see the frightful reality of disease, famine, and disasters against which we have only a nominal defense, Freud assumed that we postulate a supernatural being who can deliver us.

To illustrate that, picture in your mind a native who lives on a volcanic island. Suddenly he hears rumblings, and the ground begins to shake. He walks outside his hut and sees lava blowing out of the top of the volcano. He realizes that shoring up his hut and comforting his wife and children won't help. Since there seems to be no way out, he resorts to looking for a supernatural being to save him from the terror of nature.

Another reason for inventing God, Freud claimed, is our fear of relationships. Because people often feel used by others, Freud assumed it was natural to conjure up a divine umpire—a cosmic God with a super-whistle who ultimately stops play and penalizes people for what they have done. He made the commonsense observation that we all want someone who can right the wrongs of injustice.

Freud also attributed this supposed invention of God to the fear of death. He claimed that we want a heavenly Father who will take us to a happy place, which we call heaven. It's hard to face the fact that we might cease to exist forever.

What about Freud's claims? What are we to think of them? To begin with, his view of religion is rather simplistic. It's human nature to prefer that God *not* exist. The first thing Adam and Eve did after they sinned was to hide from God (Gen. 3:8). To be free from the God who calls sinners into accountability has been a constant goal of humanity throughout history.

The apostle Paul stated that everyone knows of God's existence "because that which is known about God is evident within them; for God made it evident to them. For since the creation of the world His invisible attributes, His eternal power and divine nature, have been clearly seen, being understood through what has been made, so that they are without excuse" (Rom. 1:19-20). This knowledge of God is planted within each person, and the fact of God's existence is abundantly evident in creation.

However, even though every man and woman on earth knows of God's existence, they do "not see fit to acknowledge God any longer" (v. 28). They reject God's self-revelation and refuse to acknowledge His glorious attributes. Freud had it wrong: People do not wish to invent the true God; instead, they wish to deny His existence.

Furthermore, a careful examination of world religions shows that the gods spawned by them are rarely of the delivering kind, but usually have an oppressive nature that needs continual appeasement. Women in India who drown their babies in the Ganges River don't think of their god as a savior, but as a fearful ogre whom they must appease. The gods of false religions are not protecting gods; they are gods to be feared. If people invent gods, they surely invent the wrong kinds! In fact, Psalm 106 makes it clear that such "gods" are actually "demons" (vv. 36-37; cf. Ps. 96:5).

THE ONLY TRUE GOD

In contrast to Sigmund Freud are believers who accept the existence of God by faith. The beginning of faith is this: "He who comes to God must believe that He is" (Heb. 11:6). It involves more than just believing there is a God. It means believing in the only true God as revealed in Scripture.

In the Old Testament the Lord taught Job a lesson about faith by saying:

> *Where were you when I laid the*
> *   foundation of the earth?*
> *Tell Me, if you have understanding,*
> *Who set its measurements, since you know?*
> *Or who stretched the line on it?*
> *On what were its bases sunk?*
> *Or who laid its cornerstone,*
> *When the morning stars sang together,*
> *And all the sons of God shouted for joy?*
> —JOB 38:4-7

The Lord was saying, "Job, you don't know anything except what you know by faith. You weren't around. You don't have any answers except the answers I give you—and you either believe them or you don't." Having faith is believing that what God says is true. The content of the Christian faith is God's revealed Word.

Some people want to prove the existence of God through science. As valuable as science is, it has its limits. Paul Little, a leader within Inter-Varsity Christian Fellowship and later associate professor of evangelism at Trinity Evangelical Divinity School, pointed out:

It can be said with equal emphasis that you can't "prove" Napoleon by the scientific method. The reason lies in the nature of history itself and in the limitations of the scientific method. In order for something to be "proved" by the scientific method, it must be repeatable. One cannot announce a new finding to the world on the basis of a single experiment.

But history in its very nature is nonrepeatable. No man can "rerun" the beginning of the universe or bring Napoleon back or repeat the assassination of Lincoln or the crucifixion of Jesus Christ. But the fact that these events can't be "proved" by repetition does not disprove their reality as events. (*Know Why You Believe* [Downers Grove, Ill.: InterVarsity, 1968], p. 8)

You can't apply the scientific method to everything; it just doesn't work. You can't put love, justice, or anger in a test tube, but they're obviously real nonetheless. Although you can't prove the existence of God from science, there are abundant scientific and other rational evidences that make it reasonable to believe in God and His Word. Nevertheless, when you come right down to it, the Christian life boils down to faith. A person finally has to say, "I believe."

As believers, we acknowledge that God exists. But do we know the God who exists? Do we know what He is like? If we are to learn of Him, we must turn to Scripture, for that is where He has revealed Himself to us.

GOD IS A PERSONAL BEING

Albert Einstein admitted the existence of a cosmic force in the universe but concluded that it is unknowable (*Cosmic Religion* [New York: Covici, Friede, 1931], pp. 47-48). He was sadly mistaken. God *is* knowable, for He said, "You will seek Me and find Me when you search for Me with all your heart" (Jer. 29:13). The apostle Peter said to believers, "Grow in the grace and *knowledge* of our Lord and Savior Jesus Christ" (2 Pet. 3:18, emphasis added). He wouldn't have said that if it weren't possible to do so.

God is knowable because He is a personal Being. The Bible uses personal titles to describe Him, such as *Father, Shepherd, Friend,* and *Counselor.* The Bible also uses personal pronouns to refer to God. The Hebrew and Greek texts refer to God as "He," never as "it." We also know that God is a personal Being because He thinks, acts, feels, and speaks—He communicates.

GOD IS A SPIRITUAL BEING

That God's essential nature is spiritual is implied in the statement, "God is not a man" (Num. 23:19). Jesus declared, "God is spirit, and those who worship Him must worship in spirit and truth" (John 4:24). What does "spirit" mean? Theologian Charles Hodge explained it this way:

> It is impossible . . . to overestimate the importance of the truth contained in the simple proposition, God is a Spirit. It is involved in that proposition that God is immaterial. None of the properties of matter can be predicated of Him. He is not extended or divisible, or compounded, or visible, or tangible. He has neither bulk nor form. . . . In revealing, therefore, that God is a Spirit, the Bible reveals to us that no attribute of matter can be predicated of the divine essence. (*Systematic Theology,* abridged edition [Grand Rapids, Mich.: Baker, 1988], pp. 138-139)

Although God is not material, the Bible does describe Him in a material way:

> *The eyes of the LORD . . . range to and fro throughout the earth.*
> —ZECH. 4:10

> *Is My hand so short that it cannot ransom?*
> —ISA. 50:2

You have a strong arm, Your hand is mighty, Your right hand is exalted.

—Ps. 89:13

We call those descriptions *anthropomorphisms*. The word is derived from two Greek words: *anthropos* (man) and *morphe* (form). God refers to Himself in human form not because He is material, but to accommodate our finite understanding.

That God is a spiritual being means His essence is invisible. The apostle Paul wrote, "Now to the King eternal, immortal, invisible, the only God, be honor and glory forever and ever. Amen" (1 Tim. 1:17). Now in the Old Testament God did represent Himself by the *Shekinah*—the divine light, fire, and cloud. And in the New Testament He represented Himself in the human form of Jesus Christ, who was fully God and fully man (John 1:14, 18). But such visible revelations did not reveal the totality or fullness of God's essential nature.

GOD IS ONE

In the Old Testament we find the shocking statement, "You are gods" (Ps. 82:6). Does that mean there really are many gods? No. God was speaking to human judges of the nation of Israel. As representatives of God, they were given the high honor of judging the people on His behalf. The reference is to their office, not to their essence. That is obvious from verse 7, which says that they, like all men, were subject to death.

There is only one true God, not many. Moses made that clear when he said, "Hear, O Israel! The LORD is our God, the LORD is one!" (Deut. 6:4) That truth was central to Israel's religious convictions. Because they lived in the midst of polytheistic societies, it was vital that they give their allegiance to the one true God. God said, "I am the first and I am the last, and there is no God besides Me" (Isa. 44:6). God is a jealous God (Exod. 20:5), which means He alone is to be worshiped.

In the New Testament Christ correctly identified Himself as God. He was not claiming to be another god, however, for He echoed the teaching of Moses:

> *"'Hear, O Israel! The Lord our God is one Lord; and you shall love the Lord your God with all your heart, and with all your soul, and with all your mind, and with all your strength.'"*
> —MARK 12:29-30

Christ said we are to love God with undivided commitment, while at the same time He was claiming to be that very God. If Christ were claiming to be *another* God, He never would have made that statement. He would have had to say, "Split your allegiance between the two of Us." You can love God with all you have to give because there's no other god with whom to share your love.

The oneness of God is an important doctrine Paul emphasized often. In his first letter to the Corinthians he wrote:

> *There is no God but one. For even if there are so-called gods [according to other religions] . . . for us there is but one God, the Father, from whom are all things and we exist for Him; and one Lord, Jesus Christ, by whom are all things, and we exist through Him.*
> —8:4-6

What was Paul saying? That we receive all things from both the Father and Christ. How can that be so? Because in essence they are one and the same. God is one.

The universality of the Gospel is inextricably bound to the oneness of God, for Paul wrote:

> *Is God the God of Jews only? Is He not the God of Gentiles also? Yes, of Gentiles also, since indeed God who will justify the circumcised by faith and the uncircumcised through faith is one.*
> —ROM. 3:29-30

There's only one true God, and because that is so, everyone must come to Him for salvation. Paul said, "There is one God, and one mediator also between God and men, the man Christ Jesus" (1 Tim. 2:5). The Bible makes it clear that there is only one Savior—God. He alone is the source of salvation for all people. The epistle of Titus refers to God as Savior three times—the same number of times it also refers to Jesus as Savior.

GOD IS THREE

God is one, yet exists not as two but as three distinct Persons. That is a mystery unparalleled in our experience. Some people try to explain it by using earthly illustrations. They point out that an egg is one, yet consists of three parts: a shell, a white, and a yolk. Or they note that water is one substance, yet can exist in three states: solid, liquid, and gas. Those comparisons help a little, but no illustration can do justice to the Trinity. Our majestic, Triune God is so far beyond mere eggs or water! His greatness is infinite, and we can never fully comprehend it. We must simply accept the clear teaching of Scripture. What exactly does Scripture say about the Trinity?

Old Testament Teaching on the Trinity

The Old Testament expresses the plurality of the Godhead in its opening words: "In the beginning God . . ." (Gen. 1:1). The Hebrew word translated "God" there is *Elohim*. The plural suffix, *im*, presents a singular God who is expressed as a plurality.

The plurality of the Godhead is also evident in Creation, for God said, "Let *Us* make man in *Our* image, according to *Our* likeness" (1:26, emphasis added). When the Lord was about to destroy the Tower of Babel, He said, "Come, let *Us* go down and there confuse their language, so that they will not understand one another's speech" (11:7, emphasis added).

Distinctions between the members of the Trinity are apparent in several Old Testament passages. For example, in Genesis 19 we read, "The LORD rained on Sodom and Gomorrah brimstone and fire from the LORD out of heaven" (v. 24). Furthermore, Charles Hodge points out this intriguing and often overlooked detail:

> We . . . find throughout the Old Testament constant mention made of a person to whom, though distinct from Jehovah as a person, the titles, attributes, and works of Jehovah are nevertheless ascribed. This person is called the angel of God, the angel of Jehovah, Adonai, Jehovah, and Elohim. He claims divine authority, exercises divine prerogatives, and receives divine homage. . . .
>
> Besides this we have the express testimony of the inspired writers of the New Testament that the angel of the Lord, the manifested Jehovah who led the Israelites through the wilderness and who dwelt in the temple, was Christ; that is, the angel was the Word . . . who became flesh and fulfilled the work which it was predicted the Messiah should accomplish. (*Systematic Theology*, p. 177)

Keeping that in mind, it is then clear that there are several Old Testament passages where Christ is speaking, and in some of them He mentions two other divine Persons. For example, in the book of Isaiah He says:

> *"Come near to Me, listen to this:*
> *From the first I have not spoken in secret,*
> *From the time it took place, I was there.*
> *And now the LORD God has sent Me, and His Spirit."*
> —48:16

New Testament Teaching on the Trinity

The Gospel of Luke reveals that all members of the Trinity were involved in Christ's incarnation, for an angel appeared to Mary and said:

The Holy Spirit will come upon you, and the power of the Most High will overshadow you; and for that reason the holy Child shall be called the Son of God.

—1:35

The Trinity was also present at Christ's baptism, for the Holy Spirit descended on Him like a dove, and the Father said, "This is My beloved Son, in whom I am well-pleased" (Matt. 3:17). We see the Father, Son, and Holy Spirit together in the same scene.

The Trinity was also involved in the resurrection of Christ. He was raised by the power of the Father (Rom. 6:4; Gal. 1:1; 1 Pet. 1:3), the Son Himself (John 10:18), and the Holy Spirit (Rom. 8:11).

Full involvement of the Trinity is also apparent in Christ's atonement, for the author of Hebrews said, "How much more will the blood of Christ, who through the eternal Spirit offered Himself without blemish to God, cleanse your conscience from dead works to serve the living God?" (9:14). Christ offered Himself as a sinless sacrifice to the Father, and the Holy Spirit empowered Him to do so. The apostle Peter echoed that truth, saying that we as believers "are chosen according to the fore-knowledge of God the Father, by the sanctifying work of the Spirit, to obey Jesus Christ" (1 Pet. 1:1-2).

All the members of the Trinity are involved in securing our salvation. God the Father establishes us in Christ (2 Cor. 1:21-22); Christ ensures that we will be found blameless (1 Cor. 1:7-8); and the Holy Spirit seals us with His promise of our heavenly inheritance (Eph. 1:13).

Evidence of the Trinity is also found in the Great Commission, for Christ said we are to "make disciples of all the nations, baptizing them in the name of the Father and the Son and the Holy Spirit" (Matt. 28:19). Baptism demonstrates the believer's union not only with Christ, but with the entire Godhead. Notice that the verse doesn't say, "baptizing them in the name of the Father, and the name of the Son, and the name of the Holy Spirit." Neither does it say, "In the names of the Father, the Son, and the Holy Spirit." The mystery of the Trinity is that there's one name and three Persons. Since "name" refers to all that a person is and does, it speaks here of all that God is and does as the Trinity.

Paul often alluded to the Trinity in his New Testament letters. To the Romans he wrote that the Holy Spirit is both "the Spirit of God" and "the Spirit of Christ" (8:9). The Holy Spirit has the same relationship with the Father that He has with the Son.

Paul's first letter to the Corinthians mentions the members of the Trinity alongside one another: "Now there are varieties of gifts, but the same Spirit. And there are varieties of ministries, and the same Lord. There are varieties of effects, but the same God" (1 Cor. 12:4-6). Later in his second letter he mentions Them together again: "The grace of the Lord Jesus Christ, and the love of God, and the fellowship of the Holy Spirit, be with you all" (2 Cor. 13:14).

He also wrote to the Thessalonians, "We should always give thanks to God for you, brethren beloved by the Lord, because God has chosen you from the beginning for salvation through sanctification by the Spirit" (2 Thess. 2:13).

Many times the interworking of the Trinity is beyond our comprehension. For example, Christ said, "I will ask the Father, and He will give you another Helper, that He may be with you forever; that is the Spirit of Truth" (John 14:16-17). That verse indicates that the Father sent the Spirit. Later Christ said, "When the Helper comes, whom I will send to you from the Father, that is the Spirit of truth, who proceeds from the Father, He will testify about Me" (15:26). That verse indicates that the Son sent the Spirit. We can conclude that both the Father and the Son were responsible in sending the Holy Spirit. But the exact nature of the relationship among the members of the Trinity remains a mystery.

Who can comprehend the Trinity? God is three in one and one in three—an eternal mystery. J. I. Packer wrote:

> Here we face the most dizzying and unfathomable truth of all, the truth of the Trinity. . . . What should we make of it? In itself, the divine trinity is a mystery, a transcendent fact which passes our understanding. . . .
>
> How the one eternal God is eternally both singular and plural, how Father, Son, and Spirit are personally distinct yet essentially one . . . is more than we can know, and any attempt to "explain" it—to dispel the mystery by reasoning, as distinct from confessing it from Scripture—is bound to falsify it. Here, as elsewhere, our God is too big for his creatures' little minds. (*I Want to Be a Christian* [Wheaton, Ill.: Tyndale, 1977], pp. 29-30)

We cannot comprehend this Triune God, but we do know that He is a Father who loves us, a Son who died for us, and a Spirit who comforts us. In the following chapters we will study other characteristics of God. But we needed to start here, for the Trinity is the most unfathomable truth of Scripture. It humbles us in preparation for what is to come.

Pray that this majestic God will reveal Himself more fully to you through the Scriptures—and long to know Him with all your heart!

2

OUR FAITHFUL,
UNCHANGING GOD

The following article was featured on the front page of the *Los Angeles Times* a few years back:

> At a recent white-tie dinner in Washington, Russian Ambassador Vladimir Lukin found himself seated across from CIA Director Robert M. Gates. The envoy from the former "evil empire" turned amiably to his dinner companion and said, "So when are we going to get together and make some new rules for spying on each other?"
>
> Gates . . . expressed guarded interest in the idea. He encouraged Lukin to discuss it with Yevgeny Primakov, the head of the Russian intelligence service that took over the espionage functions of the now-defunct Soviet KGB.
>
> But don't expect U.S. and Russian spooks to join hands and agree anytime soon on the kind of spying they will do and will not do in each other's country. Suspicion runs too deep. . . .
>
> Even among the friendliest of intelligence services, there are still layers and layers of secrets. All understandings are tacit, and behavior is moderated more by the threat of getting caught than by any firm agreements. (John M. Broder, "Spies Who Won't Come in from the Cold War," May 17, 1992, pp. A1, A12)

Just as there is distrust between nations, so there is distrust between individuals. In our day we are well on our way to trusting no one. People are learning not to trust anyone but themselves, realizing by firsthand experience that trust is an elusive virtue. Promises often mean little or nothing, and lying has become commonplace in our society.

In the midst of the confusion that lying and distrust always bring, people look for something or someone in which to place their trust. Many put their trust in the gods of man-made religions. Some put their trust in self-proclaimed healers. I heard of a mother who took her young son to a so-called healer in the hopes of having his crippled legs straightened. She was told to take off her son's braces and never put them on again. A few weeks later, after much pain, emergency surgery was done to save the boy's legs from amputation.

False teachers have always been around to steal the heart, trust, and money of people. Not too many years ago a Los Angeles minister conducted a television campaign pretending to raise money for missionary work. After raising a considerable sum, he left town and disappeared.

False teachers who are both deceived and are deceivers abound. There are teachers with high academic credentials from prestigious seminaries who preach heretical philosophies and theology. Furthermore, many people go to churches that claim to teach about Christ but in reality deny the truth. As a result, the people learn nothing about the Christ of Scripture. With lies and deception all around us, who can we trust?

The only One we can trust without reservation is God. Because of His character, He "cannot lie" (Titus 1:2). Whatever He says or does is absolute truth. He has no ability to contradict Himself. When He makes a promise, He can't help but keep it. He never deviates from His will or His Word.

Because God is trustworthy, we can be sure that He is always faithful toward His own children. That's why you can trust Him no matter what happens. Although you may be experiencing adversity, you can *know* that He is reliable.

Do you know God like that? Have you acknowledged His faithfulness on your behalf?

GOD'S TRUSTWORTHY CHARACTER

We see God's faithfulness clearly illustrated in the life of Abraham. Abraham, whose original name was Abram, grew up in a pagan environment—in Ur, an ancient Chaldean city of Mesopotamia, between the Tigris and Euphrates Rivers. It was a fertile land, where the Garden of Eden was probably located and where the great city of Babylon was eventually built. He was a descendant of Shem, one of Noah's three sons, but for many generations his family worshiped false gods (Josh. 24:2).

Abraham's Journey

One day God spoke to Abraham and commanded him to go to Canaan. The writer of Hebrews says, "By faith Abraham, when he was called, obeyed by going out to a place which he was to receive for an inheritance; and he went out, not knowing where he was going" (11:8). The Greek word for "knowing" means "to fix one's attention on" or "to put one's thoughts on." He left for a foreign land, not even putting his thoughts on where he was going.

Furthermore, he had no guarantee apart from God's Word that He would get there. His pilgrimage of faith led him to forsake his birthplace, home, and estate. He severed family ties, left loved ones, and abandoned present security for future uncertainty. Why did he obey and leave? Because he knew God is trustworthy.

Abraham's Sacrifice

The brilliant theologian Jonathan Edwards movingly wrote:

I have been before God, and have given myself, all that I am and have, to God; so that I am not, in any respect, my own. I can challenge no right in this understanding, this will, these affections, which are in me. Neither have I any right to this body, or any of its members—no right to this tongue, these hands, these feet; no right to these senses, these eyes, these ears, this smell, or this taste. I have given myself clear away, and have not retained any thing as my own. (*The Works of Jonathan Edwards*, Vol. 1 [Carlisle, Penn.: The Banner of Truth Trust, 1990, reprint], p. xxv)

Edwards offered himself completely to God, willing to obey Him unreservedly. We see the same attitude in Abraham, as revealed in this dramatic scene:

God tested Abraham, and said to him, "Abraham!"

And he said, "Here I am."

He said, "Take now your son, your only son, whom you love, Isaac, and go to the land of Moriah, and offer him there as a burnt offering on one of the mountains of which I will tell you."

So Abraham rose early in the morning and saddled his donkey, and took two of his young men with him and Isaac his son; and he split wood for the burnt offering, and arose and went to the place of which God had told him.

On the third day Abraham raised his eyes and saw the place from a distance. Abraham said to his young men, "Stay here with the donkey, and I and the lad will go there; and we will worship and return to you."

Abraham took the wood of the burnt offering and laid it on Isaac his son, and he took in his hand the fire and the knife. So the two of them walked on together.

Isaac spoke to Abraham his father and said, "My father!"

And he said, "Here I am, my son."

And he said, "Behold, the fire and the wood, but where is the lamb for the burnt offering?"

Abraham said, "God will provide for Himself the lamb for the burnt offering, my son."

So the two of them walked on together. Then they came to the place of which God had told him; and Abraham built the altar there and arranged the wood, and bound his son Isaac and laid him on the altar on top of the wood. Abraham stretched out his hand and took the knife to slay his son.

But the angel of the LORD called to him from heaven and said, "Abraham, Abraham!"

And he said, "Here I am."

He said, "Do not stretch out your hand against the lad, and do nothing to him; for now I know that you fear God, since you have not withheld your son, your only son, from Me."

Then Abraham raised his eyes and looked, and behold, behind him a ram caught in the thicket by his horns; and Abraham went and took the ram and offered him up for a burnt offering in the place of his son.

—GEN. 22:1-13

What a tremendous act of trust! God had already promised that Abraham's posterity would grow to the size of a nation and be His special people (12:2; 15:2-5), that the land to which God had brought Abraham would be that nation's homeland (13:14-17), and that his posterity would be a blessing to the world (12:2-3; 18:18).

Abraham "believed in the LORD; and He reckoned it to him as righteousness" (15:6). That is, Abraham believed that God would fulfill His covenant promises and do what He said. He knew, as we should, that the Lord is trustworthy and faithful to His Word.

But how could Abraham expect the promises to be fulfilled if he were to offer Isaac as a sacrifice? Abraham "considered that God is able to raise people even from the dead" (Heb. 11:19). He knew God would keep His promises somehow, even by a miracle if necessary. Abraham's faith was not blind, for he had seen God's trustworthy character and integrity on display time and time again. His faith was well placed.

GOD'S FAITHFULNESS TO HIS COVENANT

Not long after God created Adam and Eve, they decided to disobey Him. They ate the fruit from the tree of the knowledge of good and evil and fell, as did the rest of creation. The whole earth was cursed as a result. The parents of the human race lost their fellowship with God and were exiled from Eden.

Soon after that, the first murder was committed, and things went rapidly downhill from there. Corruption, violence, polygamy, idolatry, incest, lying, stealing, adultery, and every other kind of sin became common and increasingly worse. Humanity became so debauched that God destroyed everyone on the face of the earth except for the eight in Noah's family. In the generations after the Flood, however, people continued to flee from God.

Yet God did not give up on humanity. It was His eternal plan that some would worship and serve Him. Abraham was a part of that plan. He was to be the progenitor of the nation Israel, which was to bring salvation to the world through the Messiah.

Abraham, however, was only a responder to the divine plan; that is, God did not choose him to be a part of His divine plan because of any particular merit, quality, or virtue on his part.

God made His choice according to His sovereign pleasure and will. Abraham would become the father of a mighty nation, and in him all nations of the earth would be blessed simply because the Lord said, "I have chosen him" (Gen. 18:19).

The Lord certified His promise to Abraham through a covenant. In the manner of ratifying covenants at that time in the Middle East, God told Abraham to cut specified animals in half and set the halves opposite each other. After the Lord caused him to fall into a deep sleep, the Lord spoke to him about His promise and then passed between the halves Himself.

Ordinarily, both parties would walk between the pieces to symbolize their mutual responsibility in fulfilling the conditions of the agreement, as if to say, "May we ourselves be cut in two if we don't keep our part of the bargain." But Abraham had no part in determining the conditions of the covenant or the ceremony that sealed it. That only God walked between the pieces signified that the total responsibility was His. Abraham was not a party to the covenant, but a recipient of it and a vehicle for its fulfillment. The conditions and obligations were God's alone.

Abraham was secure in the eternal plan of God. Why? Because God is true to His Word and faithful to fulfill His covenant promises. In all the universe only He can say, "Surely, just as I have intended so it has happened, and just as I have planned so it will stand" (Isa. 14:24).

GOD'S UNALTERABLE PLAN OF REDEMPTION

God's sovereign choice is the theme of Romans 9. As an illustration, Paul wrote about Jacob and Esau. Although they "were not yet born, and had not done anything good or bad, so that God's purpose according to His choice would stand, not because of works but because of Him who calls, it was said . . . 'The older will serve the younger'" (vv. 11-12).

As in the case with Abraham, it is God alone and not anything a person does that brings about salvation. God has purposed to love His own, and nothing can violate that plan. When He designs His sovereign purposes, He carries them out. His plans never fail, for He is faithful to His Word.

Isaac and Jacob were not the only beneficiaries of God's plan. Paul wrote:

> They are not all Israel who are descended from Israel; nor are they all children because they are Abraham's descendants, but: "Through Isaac your descendants will be named." That is, it is not the children of the flesh who are children of God, but the children of the promise are regarded as descendants.
>
> —vv. 6-8

His point was that Abraham is the spiritual father of all who believe (cf. Rom. 4:11-12). He was referring to people's faith, not their racial heritage. In his letter to the Galatians, he says it this way: "Be sure that it is those who are of faith that are sons of Abraham" (3:7). We who believe in Christ as Savior and Lord are as secure as Abraham because we exercise the same faith he did.

As true sons of Abraham, we are secure in the Lord's plan of redemption. After all, whom God "foreknew, He also predestined to become conformed to the image of His Son, so that He would be the firstborn among many brethren; and these whom He predestined, He also called; and these whom He called, He also justified; and these whom He justified, He also glorified" (Rom. 8:29-30).

The believer does nothing to secure his or her salvation. According to God's own purpose, He secures it for us. The believer cannot secure it and certainly cannot keep it. But in His faithfulness, God does both. (I explored that issue further in my book *Saved Without a Doubt* [Wheaton, Ill.: Victor, 1992].)

Why does God choose us for salvation and conform us to the likeness of His Son? Because it is part of His sovereign, wise plan to do so. We can be sure He will never alter or annul His eternal plan, for He is always faithful to fulfill His promises.

GOD'S UNFAILING OATH

In Old Testament times, it was common for a person to make an oath by invoking the power of something or someone greater than himself or herself. For the Jewish people, that higher power was God (cf. Gen. 14:22; 21:23-24; 24:3). If someone made such an oath, he or she was responsible to keep it.

God, however, does not need to make such an oath. He is Truth itself, and there is no higher power. His Word is for us to accept, not doubt. Nevertheless, God did guarantee His promise to Abraham with an oath:

> *For when God made the promise to Abraham, since He could swear by no one greater, He swore by Himself, saying, "I will surely bless you and I will surely multiply you." And so, having patiently waited, he obtained the promise. For men swear by one greater than themselves, and with them an oath given as confirmation is an end of every dispute.*
>
> *In the same way God, desiring even more to show to the heirs of the promise the unchangeableness of His purpose, interposed with an oath, so that by two unchangeable things in which it is impossible for God to lie, we who have taken refuge would have strong encouragement to take hold of the hope set before us.*
>
> —HEB. 6:13-18

God's oath, of course, was not given to make His promise more secure, but to accommodate people's weak faith. God descended to our level to provide us with greater assurance.

The writer of Hebrews says there are "two unchangeable things in which it is impossible for God to lie" (v. 18). The Greek word for "unchangeable" was used in relation to wills. Once properly made, a will is unchangeable by anyone but its maker.

What two things are unchangeable here? God's covenant promise and His oath. God declared both to be unchangeable, even to the point of staking His own reputation on it. His will cannot be switched, transposed, or altered. Can we be sure? Yes, because He cannot lie. He made this commitment to provide strong encouragement and confidence for all who flee to Him as their Refuge and Savior.

God added yet another reason for believers to trust Him. In Hebrews 6 the writer concluded:

> *This hope we have as an anchor of the soul, a hope both sure and steadfast and one which enters within the veil, where Jesus has entered as a forerunner for us, having become a high priest forever according to the order of Melchizedek.*
>
> —vv. 19-20

As our High Priest, Christ serves as the anchor of our soul, the One who will forever keep us from drifting away from God. Commentator Homer Kent wrote:

> This anchor is secure because it is unbending. It is sure to hold because its flukes are strong and cannot be twisted out of shape nor broken. In like manner Christ in His own person is absolutely reliable and fully worthy of our trust. (*The Epistle to the Hebrews* [Grand Rapids, Mich.: Baker, 1972], p. 122)

We can trust God not only because Christ is the anchor of our soul, but also because He has entered the inner part of the veil. The phrase "within the veil" was a reference to the most sacred place in the temple, the holy of holies. Inside the holy of holies was the ark of the covenant, which signified the glory of God. Once a year, on the Day of Atonement, the high priest would enter the holy of holies to make atonement for the sins of God's people.

Under the New Covenant, however, atonement was made once for all time by Christ's sacrifice on the cross (Heb. 9:12).

As our forerunner, Christ entered heaven—the inner part of the veil. In God's mind, our soul is secure in heaven with Christ.

The absolute security that God provides is almost incomprehensible. Not only are our souls anchored within the impregnable, inviolable heavenly sanctuary, but Christ stands guard over them as well. Surely we can entrust our souls to this supremely faithful God!

GOD'S UNCHANGING CHARACTER

The faithfulness of God is intertwined with His immutable character. In the book of Malachi, God said of Himself, "I, the LORD, do not change" (3:6). With Him "there is no variation or shifting shadow" (Jas. 1:17).

Change is either for the better or for the worse. Yet both are inconceivable in God. In his book *The Attributes of God,* writer and teacher A. W. Pink wrote:

> [God] cannot change for the better, for He is already perfect; and being perfect, He cannot change for the worse. Altogether unaffected by anything outside Himself, improvement or deterioration is impossible. He is perpetually the same. ([Grand Rapids, Mich.: Baker, 1975], p. 37)

Nevertheless, biblical passages that imply God can change confuse some people. For example, Genesis 6:6-7: "The LORD was sorry that He had made man on the earth, and He was grieved in His heart, and the LORD said, 'I will blot out man whom I have created from the face of the land, from man to animals to creeping things and to birds of the sky; for I am sorry that I have made them.'" But think about this: Whose character changed? Not God's. He created people to do good, but instead, they changed and chose to do evil.

In the book of Jonah we see another often misunderstood passage. When God saw the inhabitants of Nineveh turn from their sin, He "relented concerning the calamity which He had declared He would bring upon them. And He did not do it" (3:10). But again, who changed? Not God. He showed mercy to Nineveh not because He Himself repented, but because the people did.

Louis Berkhof addressed the issue this way:

> There is change round about Him [God], change in the relations of men to Him, but there is no change in His Being, His attributes, His purpose, His motives of action, or His promises. . . . If Scripture speaks of His repenting, changing His intention, and altering His relation to sinners when they repent, we should remember that this is only an anthropopathic way of speaking. In reality the change is not in God, but in man and in man's relations to God. (*Systematic Theology* [Grand Rapids, Mich.: Eerdmans, 1941], p. 59)

The way a person stands before God dictates what happens to him or her. You can't blame the sun for melting wax and hardening clay. The difference is in the substance of those objects, not in the sun. God never changes. He will continue to reward good and to punish evil. Moses wrote of God's unchanging character this way:

> *God is not a man, that He should lie,*
> *Nor a son of man, that He should repent;*
> *Has He said, and will He not do it?*
> *Or has He spoken, and will He not make it good?*
> —NUM. 23:19

God's unchanging character sets Him apart from everyone and everything. The heavens, for example, are subject to change. They move about, following their courses. The book of Revelation gives us a drastic picture of the extreme changes the heavens will undergo until fire eventually dissolves them. The stars will fall, the sun will go out, the moon will turn a bloody hue, and the heavens will roll up like a scroll.

The earth also is subject to change. People have been changing the face of the earth with their bulldozers and changing the atmosphere with pollution. The book of Revelation says that in the end-times both people and plant life will die, and the seas will be polluted. The earth was changed once by a flood; it will be changed again when it is consumed with intense heat (2 Pet. 3:6-7).

The ungodly are subject to change. Unbelievers now think they have a happy or at least an acceptable life. But one day they will realize that an eternity without God is a tragic existence. Angels are also subject to change, for some "did not keep their own domain, but abandoned their proper abode" (Jude 6). Those beings are demons.

Even believers change. There are times when our love for Christ burns and we obey Him, but there are other times when it smolders and we disobey. On the one hand, David trusted the Lord as his Rock and Refuge (2 Sam. 22:3); on the other hand, he feared for his life, saying, "I will perish one day by the hand of Saul" (1 Sam. 27:1). Everyone and everything in the universe changes—except God!

What does the unchanging character of God mean to us as Christians? Comfort. As A. W. Pink pointed out:

> Human nature cannot be relied upon; but God can! However unstable I may be, however fickle my friends may prove, God changes not. If He varied as we do, if He willed one thing today and another tomorrow, if He were controlled by caprice, who could confide in Him?
>
> But, all praise to His glorious name, He is ever the same. His purpose is fixed, His will is stable, His word is sure. Here then is a rock on which we may fix our feet, while the mighty torrent is sweeping away everything around us. The permanence of God's character guarantees the fulfillment of His promises. (*The Attributes of God,* p. 39)

God's promises include a salvation for believers that is eternal. That means He will faithfully manifest His love, forgiveness, mercy, and grace toward us forever! God reassuringly says, "The mountains may be removed and the hills may shake, but My lovingkindness will not be removed from you, and My covenant of peace will not be shaken" (Isa. 54:10).

This is the faithful, unchanging God you can trust completely. He will always be true to His Word and will fulfill all His promises. It's no wonder Christ said, "Have faith in God" (Mark 11:22). He was saying, "You can trust God. You can put your life in His hands." May the Lord help you do just that!

3

OUR HOLY GOD

Robert Murray McCheyne was a man with a great passion for God. Shortly after his conversion, he made the following entries in his diary:

June 30, 1832:
   Much carelessness, sin and sorrow. "O wretched man that I am! Who shall deliver me from this body of sin and death?" Enter thou, my soul, into the rock, and hide thee in the dust for fear of the Lord and the glory of His majesty.

July 3, 1832:
   This last bitter root of worldliness that has so often betrayed me has this night so grossly, that I cannot but regard it as God's chosen way to make me loathe and forsake it for ever. I would vow; but it is much more like a weakly worm to pray. Sit in the dust, O my soul!

July 22, 1832:
   Had this evening a more complete understanding of that self-emptying and abasement with which it is necessary to come to Christ—a denying of self, trampling it under foot— a recognizing of the complete righteousness and justice of God, that could do nothing else with us but condemn us utterly, and thrust us down to lowest hell—a feeling that, even in hell, we should rejoice in His sovereignty, and say that all was rightly done. (Andrew A. Bonar, *Memoir and Remains of*

Robert Murray McCheyne [Carlisle, Penn.: The Banner of Truth Trust, 1973], pp. 18-19)

McCheyne had a profound sense of his own sin and a high view of God's holiness. What makes his diary entries all the more remarkable is that he was only nineteen years old when he recorded them. Later he became the minister of St. Peter's Church in Dundee, Scotland. He ministered but a short seven and a half years and died at the age of twenty-nine. He left relatively few sermon notes; yet the fruitfulness of his brief life remains to this day. His biography has gone through more than a hundred editions with more than half a million copies circulated around the world. Why? One reason is that the young Scottish minister saw God as He really is.

In stark contrast, many who name Christ today have only a weak, shallow, and superficial view of God. They are caught up in a kind of self-indulgence and self-centeredness that views God only in terms of what He can do for them. They have fashioned God into a utilitarian genie.

But if we are to see God as He really is—to see Him as He is revealed in His Word—we must understand and know this fundamental fact: Our God is holy.

HOLY, HOLY, HOLY

Holiness is arguably the most significant of all God's attributes. When the angels worship in heaven, they do not say, "Eternal, eternal, eternal," or "Faithful, faithful, faithful," or "Wise, wise, wise," or "Mighty, mighty, mighty." They say, "Holy, Holy, Holy, is the Lord God, the Almighty" (Rev. 4:8; cf. Isa. 6:3).

In his classic book *The Existence and Attributes of God,* Stephen Charnock noted that God's holiness "is the crown of all His attributes, the life of all His decrees, the brightness of all His actions. Nothing is decreed by Him, nothing is acted by Him, but what is worthy of the dignity, and becoming the honour, of this attribute" ([Minneapolis: Klock & Klock, 1977 reprint], p. 452). The holiness of the Lord is awesome, fearful, and majestic. David wrote, "Holy and awesome is His name" (Ps. 111:9). In her song of thanksgiving Hannah prayed, "There is no one holy like the LORD, indeed, there is no one besides You" (1 Sam. 2:2). Moses and the sons of Israel said of God, "Who is like You, majestic in holiness?" (Exod. 15:11).

What does it mean to be holy? Charles Hodge explains:

> This is a general term for the moral excellence of God. . . . Holiness, on the one hand, implies entire freedom from moral evil and, on the other, absolute moral perfection. Freedom from impurity is the primary idea of the word. To sanctify is to cleanse; to be holy is to be clean. Infinite purity, even more than infinite knowledge or infinite power, is the object of reverence. (*Systematic Theology*, abridged edition [Grand Rapids, Mich.: Baker, 1988], pp. 150-151)

Simply put, God is without sin. He doesn't conform to some holy standard—He *is* the standard. He never does anything wrong. There are no degrees to His holiness, for He is perfectly holy.

Between God and us is a gulf separating holiness from unholiness. He is holy; we are unholy. As a result, we will be shaken to the roots of our being when we see ourselves in comparison to His holiness. That's a frightening thought since holiness is the standard for existing in His presence. It's why God "did not spare angels when they sinned, but cast them into hell and committed them to pits of darkness, reserved for judgment" (2 Pet. 2:4). Similarly, the unrepentant sinner is sent "into the eternal fire which has been prepared for the devil and his angels" (Matt. 25:41).

How can we be holy? By exercising faith in the Lord Jesus Christ. Through Christ's atoning work on the cross, God imputes holiness to those who believe in Him. Paul said to the Corinthians, "You were washed, you were sanctified [made holy], you were justified in the name of the Lord Jesus Christ" (1 Cor. 6:11, NIV).

GOD'S HATRED OF SIN

A good way to understand God's holiness is to see it in contrast to His hatred of sin. We can much more readily identify with that since we are so familiar with sin.

In the book of Amos God said to His people, "I hate, I reject your festivals, nor do I delight in your solemn assemblies. Even though you offer up to Me burnt offerings and your grain offerings, I will not accept them; and I will not even look at the peace offerings of your fatlings. Take away from Me the noise of your songs; I will not even listen to the sound of your harps" (5:21-23). God had instituted ceremonial and sacrificial ordinances for the people to follow, but they performed them with impure hearts. God hates that. David wrote, "The LORD is righteous, He loves righteousness" (Ps. 11:7). Sin is the object of His displeasure, but He loves holiness. He doesn't want people doing even right things with the wrong attitude.

Although God is holy and hates sin, He still redeemed us. He knows and despises our sin; yet He loves us. God's holiness, omniscience, and love all act in harmony. To better understand that kind of love, consider what it might be like to have cancer. If your body were infected with cancer, you would love your body but hate the cancer. You would do everything you could to preserve your body—to keep it strong and care for it. And you would do everything you could to destroy the cancer. Similarly, God loves the believer but despises his or her sin. He never wills for anyone to sin or tempts anyone to sin (Jas. 1:13-14). He gives us freedom of choice, but so often we choose to sin.

THE GREATEST EXPRESSION OF HOLINESS

We see God's holiness expressed throughout Scripture. It was evident from the very beginning in creation, for Solomon said, "God made men upright" (Eccl. 7:29). He made us to be holy.

God's holiness is also evident in His moral law. The apostle

Paul wrote that "the Law is holy, and the commandment is holy and righteous and good" (Rom. 7:12). The Bible reveals that its author, God, is likewise holy, righteous, and good.

In addition, the sacrificial law reveals the holiness of God. When God instructed the Israelites to offer animals as sacrifices for sin, He was demonstrating that death is the result of sin. That communicates that God is so holy that He cannot be approached without a substitutionary sacrifice for sin (see Heb. 9:22).

God's holiness is also expressed in His judgment of sin. Paul wrote of Christ's Second Coming, "The Lord Jesus will be revealed from heaven with His mighty angels in flaming fire, dealing out retribution to those who do not know God and to those who do not obey the gospel of our Lord Jesus" (2 Thess. 1:7-8). Jude says the Lord will come "to execute judgment upon all, and to convict all the ungodly of all their ungodly deeds which they have done in an ungodly way, and of all the harsh things which ungodly sinners have spoken against Him" (v. 15). God's judgment on sin is a reflection of His holiness because He, by His very nature, *must* punish sin.

The greatest expression of God's holiness was His sending His own Son to die on a cross to make salvation possible. He paid the highest price imaginable to satisfy His absolute holiness. The author of Hebrews said of Christ, "At the consummation of the ages He has been manifested to put away sin by the sacrifice of Himself" (9:26). For the sake of satisfying God's holiness, Christ willingly bore the sins of humanity and died a sacrificial death.

A CALL TO HOLINESS

Isaiah the prophet knew well of the Lord's awesome, majestic holiness. He spoke for God to common people as well as to kings. He prophesied during the reign of four monarchs over a period of sixty years. His ministry occurred during a time of great crisis, chaos, and moral decadence—a time when God's people had turned their backs on Him.

One of the kings who reigned during Isaiah's ministry was Uzziah. He reigned for a long time and was a successful ruler. He turned Jerusalem into a fortified city so that it was well equipped to defend itself. He developed agriculture and commerce for the nation until it became extremely prosperous. As a result of his leadership, the people enjoyed great peace and security.

When Uzziah looked at all of his accomplishments, however, his heart was filled with pride, and the Lord afflicted him with terminal leprosy (2 Chron. 26:16-21). Undoubtedly, a sense of panic set in among the inhabitants of Judah. When the king died, they probably said, "Uzziah provided us with a respite from all the chaos around us. Now what will happen?" They became fearful.

What especially made them afraid was that Tiglath-pileser III, the ambitious warrior-king of Assyria, suddenly appeared on the horizon in the east. His grand design was to conquer all the kingdoms between the Euphrates and Nile Rivers and establish an empire.

Isaiah called on the people to turn back to God, but instead they were caught up in a frenzy of self-indulgence, dissipation, and moral decadence. The Lord called them "to weeping, to wailing, to shaving the head and to wearing sackcloth," but instead there was "gaiety and gladness, killing of cattle and slaughtering of sheep, eating of meat and drinking of wine" (Isa. 22:12-13). The Lord was calling them to repent of their sin, but instead their attitude was, "Let us eat and drink, for tomorrow we may die."

SEEING GOD'S HOLY PRESENCE

Some of the people, however, feared God and maintained a true devotion to Him. Isaiah was among them. In the year King Uzziah died, something happened that would change Isaiah forever.

The prophet, in a vision, "saw the LORD sitting on a throne, lofty and exalted, with the train of His robe filling the temple" (Isa. 6:1). The apostle John suggested that Isaiah's vision was a preincarnate appearance of Christ (John 12:41). It pictures the Lord's majesty, holiness, glory, and power.

The Hebrew word used for "Lord" in Isaiah 6:1 (*adonay*) is emphatic and refers to God's sovereignty. Isaiah was saying to the people, "In the year we lost our human king, I saw the real King." Isaiah knew there was no reason to panic because God was still on the throne. His kingship is infinitely superior to Uzziah's or anyone else's. In the midst of a national crisis, God let Isaiah know that all was not lost.

What else did Isaiah see in his vision? Above the Lord stood angels called "seraphim." In Isaiah 6:2 we see that they have the capacity to hover around the throne of God, for they have six wings. With two wings they cover their feet. Some say they do so as a sign of humility, but perhaps there is more going on here.

When Moses saw the burning bush, the Lord called to him from the midst of it and said, "Do not come near here; remove your sandals from your feet, for the place on which you are standing is holy ground" (Exod. 3:5). The ground was not holy because of any intrinsic virtue, but because God was there. His pervasive presence sanctified the earth under His feet. Whenever the divine presence appears, everything is immediately sanctified. Similarly, the seraphim of Isaiah 6 may have covered their feet because the place where they were standing was holy ground.

The seraphim also covered their faces with two wings. Why? Since they hover over the throne of the Lord, they're exposed to His full glory. No creature can withstand that brilliant sight (see Exod. 33:20).

God is unapproachable in the sense that no one has ever seen or will ever see His full glory. Even believers can't see Him in His fullness and live. It's no wonder that after being visited by the angel of the Lord, Manoah, the father of Samson, said to his wife, "We shall surely die, for we have seen God" (Judg. 13:22).

The Lord allows proximity, but never full revelation. Even in heaven we will see only a portion of His glory. Certainly it will be a greater portion than anyone has ever seen in this world, but we won't see the incomprehensible, unimaginable glory of God in its entirety. The seraphim couldn't take it; so they covered their faces.

The most incredible thing about the seraphim, however, is not what they looked like, but what they said: "Holy, Holy, Holy, is the LORD of hosts, the whole earth is full of His glory" (Isa. 6:3). Why did the angels repeat the word *holy* three times? Some claim that's a veiled reference to the Trinity, but I think there's a better explanation. The Jewish people commonly used repetition as a literary device for the sake of emphasis. For example, Christ told Nicodemus, "Truly, truly, I say to you, unless one is born again he cannot see the kingdom of God" (John 3:3). By repetition He emphasized the importance of His statement. Similarly, the seraphim cried out, "Holy, Holy, Holy" to emphasize the supreme holiness of the Lord.

As the seraphim proclaimed God's holiness to one another, "the foundations of the thresholds trembled at the voice of him who called out, while the temple was filling with smoke" (Isa. 6:4). That was quite a dramatic scene; it must have been like an erupting volcano. Isaiah's vision is reminiscent of the Lord's appearance at Mount Sinai:

> There were thunder and lightning flashes and a thick cloud upon the mountain and a very loud trumpet sound, so that all the people who were in the camp trembled. . . . The LORD descended upon it in fire; and its smoke ascended like the smoke of a furnace, and the whole mountain quaked violently.
> —EXOD. 19:16-18

In Isaiah's case, the smoke that filled the temple was either an emanation from the altar or a manifestation of the fiery presence of God. Its meaning is that God is a consuming fire and you can't toy with Him or you'll be consumed. His holiness is awesome, majestic, and fearful.

THE DEVASTATION OF GOD'S PROPHET

When Isaiah saw God for who He really is, his immediate response was, "Woe is me" (6:5). That was more than just a sign of despair. When Old Testament prophets gave pronouncements or oracles, those proclamations were often preceded by the statement, "Thus says the Lord." The pronouncement that followed could be either positive or negative. If it was positive, they'd often say, "Blessed." If it was negative, they'd say, "Woe."

In his prophecies Isaiah repeatedly used the word *woe* to refer to God's judgment on others. Christ also used it in giving this blistering rebuke to the religious leaders of His day: "Woe to you, scribes and Pharisees, hypocrites" (Matt. 23:13). It is a curse.

In Isaiah 6 we actually see a prophet of God pronouncing a curse on himself! Now Isaiah was probably the best man in the land, a true servant of God. But when he saw the holiness of God, he could see only his sin.

He then said, "I am ruined" (v. 5). The Hebrew term speaks of being lost, annihilated, or destroyed. Isaiah was saying, "I am devastated by the holiness of God." He went on to confess, "I am a man of unclean lips, and I live among a people of unclean lips." No one can stand in the presence of God without becoming profoundly and devastatingly aware of his own wretchedness. Sinclair Ferguson said:

> Isaiah was right: we are moral wrecks, and only by the grace of God are we daily preserved from total self-destruction. When . . . God's holiness breaks upon our spirits, we are delivered from all superficial and inadequate thoughts about our sanctification. We are also preserved from any cheap teaching that encourages us to think that there are short cuts by which we may more easily obtain holiness.

Holiness is not an experience; it is the re-integration of our character, the rebuilding of a ruin. It is a skilled labour, a long-term project, demanding everything God has given us for life and godliness. (*A Heart for God* [Carlisle, Penn.: The Banner of Truth Trust, 1987], p. 91)

If we don't understand the holiness of God, we won't understand our own sinfulness. And if we don't understand how heinous our sin is, we won't understand the consequences of it. Salvation will be a meaningless concept to us. To see even the smallest glimpse of God's holiness is to be devastated. Isaiah would never be the same. Never.

Although Isaiah was devastated by God's holiness, God did not leave him that way. Isaiah went on to write, "Then one of the seraphim flew to me with a burning coal in his hand, which he had taken from the altar with tongs. He touched my mouth with it and said, 'Behold, this has touched your lips; and your iniquity is taken away and your sin is forgiven'" (vv. 6-7).

Isaiah responded to the holiness of God with a broken and contrite heart. He forsook sin, embraced a holy God, and received divine forgiveness as a result.

"YOU SHALL BE HOLY"

Peter wrote, "Like the Holy One who called you [to salvation], be holy yourselves also in all your behavior; because it is written, 'You shall be holy, for I am holy'" (1 Peter 1:15-16; cf. Lev. 11:44). Since God Himself is holy, He wants His people to be holy. Living a holy life distinguishes us from the world. Positionally we are already holy in Christ, but God wants our life to match our position. That way the onlooking world will see the difference that knowing Christ makes in a person's life. Paul said, "'Everyone who names the name of the Lord is to abstain from wickedness'" (2 Tim. 2:19). If you claim to follow Christ, live a life that proves that you do.

Living a holy life will give you boldness before God. That involves regularly confessing and forsaking sin. Although the following advice from Eliphaz was insensitively given to Job, the content of what Eliphaz said is nonetheless true:

> *If you return to the Almighty, you will be restored;*
> *If you remove unrighteousness far from your tent,*
> *And place your gold in the dust . . .*
> *Then the Almighty will be your gold*
> *And choice silver to you.*
> *For then you will delight in the Almighty*
> *And lift up your face to God.*
>
> —JOB 22:23-26

You can't face God and delight in Him when there's sin in your life. Whenever there's unconfessed sin, you'll have a difficult time praying. God doesn't want that to happen to you. He wants you to be holy, even if He has to discipline you to bring that about (Heb. 12:4-11).

What should you do to become holy? Do what David did—pray for "a clean heart" (Ps. 51:9-10). Then do what David's son suggested: "He who walks with wise men will be wise, but the companion of fools will suffer harm" (Prov. 13:20). Make a habit of being around those who will influence you toward holiness.

Has the Lord taught you the extent of sin's influence in your own life? Have you ever identified with Paul's cry, as did Robert Murray McCheyne: "Wretched man that I am! Who will set me free from the body of this death?" (Rom. 7:24)? If you do not recognize the depth of your own sinfulness, you will have little appreciation for the wonder of God's grace and holiness.

4

OUR OMNISCIENT GOD

A news article entitled "Was That Xanax or Zantac?" said:

> Reports are rising of injuries and deaths due to mix-ups of
> sound-alike prescription drugs. *American Pharmacy*'s May
> issue reports 60 sets of drugs with similar names—from aceta-
> zolamide and acetohexamide (for glaucoma and diabetes,
> respectively) to Xanax and Zantac (for anxiety and ulcers).
>
> Confusion caused by drug names that slip by industry
> safeguards is compounded by physicians who pen illegible or
> incomplete prescriptions and by sloppy pharmacists. A recent
> issue of the *New England Journal of Medicine* told of two
> pharmacists who dispensed the pain reliever Norflex instead
> of the new antibiotic Norfloxacin. One patient became dizzy;
> the other hallucinated.
>
> Patients can protect themselves by asking doctors to write
> the reason a medication is being used on their prescriptions. . . .
> Then it's up to you to check the label before leaving the phar-
> macy counter. (Marc Silver, Doug Podolsky, and Anne Kates
> Smith, *U.S. News & World Report*, May 18, 1992, p. 76)

Does that scare you? Think about it: How many times have
you failed to rigorously check your prescriptions? How many
other everyday aspects of life can easily go awry from one simple mistake or oversight?

Life can be very frightening until you grasp that God is not like your well-intentioned pharmacist. With Him there are never any mix-ups. He is never confused. That's because He is omniscient. He knows everything. Isaiah wrote, "Who has directed the Spirit of the LORD, or as His counselor has informed Him? With whom did He consult and who gave Him understanding? And who taught Him in the path of justice and taught Him knowledge and informed Him of the way of understanding?" (40:13-14). The obvious answer is, no one.

Because His knowledge is infinite and perfect, God never needs to learn anything. His knowledge is vast—far beyond ours. That's why when you pray, you're not telling God anything He doesn't already know. Prayer helps you line up your desires with God's will and pleases Him because it is an act of obedience to His Word, but it does not supply God with additional information.

In *The Knowledge of the Holy*, A. W. Tozer wrote that God

knows all that can be known. And this He knows instantly and with a fullness of perfection that includes every possible item of knowledge concerning everything that exists or could have existed anywhere in the universe at any time in the past or that may exist in the centuries or ages yet unborn.

God knows . . . all causes, all thoughts, all mysteries, all enigmas, all feelings, all desires, every unuttered secret, all thrones and dominions, all personalities, all things visible and invisible in heaven and in earth. . . .

Because God knows all things perfectly, He knows no thing better than any other thing, but all things equally well. He never discovers anything, He is never surprised, never amazed. He never wonders about anything nor (except when drawing men out for their own good) does He seek information or ask questions. God is self-existent and self-contained and knows what no creature can ever know—Himself, perfectly. . . . Only the Infinite can know the infinite. ([New York: Harper & Row, 1961], pp. 62-63)

NO PLACE TO HIDE

God knows every detail of our lives. There is nothing that escapes His attention. "The very hairs of your head are all numbered," Christ said (Luke 12:7). It's not necessary for Him to count the hairs on your head because He already knows how many there are. Not even a sparrow escapes His notice (v. 6)!

Nothing can obscure what our all-knowing God sees. David wrote, "Even the darkness is not dark to You, and the night is as bright as the day. Darkness and light are alike to You" (Ps. 139:12). The darkness of night is neither a canopy that obscures God's vision nor a cloak for a person to hide his or her sin. The natural tendency of humankind is to love darkness rather than light because their deeds are evil (John 3:19). But whenever people try to hide their sin, the brilliant light of God's omniscience exposes it.

Perhaps this is the most astounding fact about God's omniscience: He knows every detail about us, and yet He still loves us. In the Old Testament God knew all about Israel's sin, yet responded with these words of love and mercy:

> *I will betroth you to Me forever;*
> *Yes, I will betroth you to Me in righteousness*
> *   and in justice,*
> *In lovingkindness and in compassion,*
> *And I will betroth you to Me in faithfulness.*
> *Then you will know the LORD.*
>
> —HOSEA 2:19-20

Similarly, "God demonstrates His own love toward us, in that while we were yet sinners, Christ died for us" (Rom. 5:8). He knew all about our sins, yet willingly gave His Son to die for us on the cross.

Our Lord Jesus Christ, God in human flesh, "searches the minds and hearts" of those who profess His name (Rev. 2:23).

Not one of our thoughts is outside His knowledge. Scripture tells us that He "knew all men" and "did not need anyone to testify concerning man, for He Himself knew what was in man" (John 2:24-25).

David said, "Even before there is a word on my tongue, behold, O LORD, You know it all" (Ps. 139:4). God knows our thoughts even before we express them. Even when we whisper our thoughts, God hears the words as if they were being broadcast.

THE FUTILITY OF HYPOCRISY

There is no secret place where you can hide from God. Know also that God sees through every false front. Christ unmasked the hypocritical Jewish religious leaders of His day by saying they were "like whitewashed tombs" (Matt. 23:27). Tombs were whitewashed to keep a traveler on his way to Jerusalem for a religious festival from inadvertently touching a tomb and becoming defiled. When a person became defiled, he had to go through ceremonial cleansing and would be excluded from participating in certain religious activities.

Although travelers coming into Jerusalem would see clean, white tombs dazzling in the sun, that didn't change what the tombs really were: the graves of dead people. The religious leaders were like those whitewashed tombs because they had a religious outward appearance, but inside they were "full of hypocrisy and lawlessness" (v. 28). They were guilty of deception, and they contaminated everyone with their teaching. Christ knows every heart, and nothing will deceive Him, not even an outward display of religion.

Sometimes it appears as though the sins of the ungodly go unnoticed by God—especially if they are prosperous and successful in the things of the world. But David had the right perspective when He said:

> *Rest in the* LORD *and wait patiently for Him;*
> *Do not fret because of him who prospers*
>   *in his way,*
> *Because of the man who carries out*
>   *wicked schemes.*
> *Cease from anger and forsake wrath;*
> *Do not fret; it leads only to evildoing.*
> *For evildoers will be cut off,*
> *But those who wait for the* LORD,
>   *they will inherit the land.*
> *Yet a little while and the wicked man*
>   *will be no more;*
> *And you will look carefully for his place,*
>   *and he will not be there.*
> *But the humble will inherit the land*
> *And will delight themselves in abundant prosperity.*
>
> —PS. 37:7-11

The prosperity of the ungodly will not last forever. There will come a day when the sin that is now hidden will be unmasked and punished.

Deep inside, the ungodly hope that God will judge them by something other than truth. They may try to hide behind their national identity, church affiliation, baptism, adherence to rules, or morality. Many people who go to church do not really know the Lord. They appear to be godly, but their hearts are like whitewashed tombs. Christ warned that many will profess to follow Him without really knowing Him (Matt. 7:22-23). The lost, whether religious or not, need to turn from their sin and trust the omniscient God as their Savior.

No one should think he or she can play games with an all-knowing God, for God "will bring every act to judgment, everything which is hidden, whether it is good or evil" (Eccl. 12:14). God knows all the facts. His judgment will be just and accurate because it will be according to truth. His perception is never distorted, for He said:

> *I, the* LORD, *search the heart,*
> *I test the mind,*
> *Even to give to each man according to his ways,*
> *According to the results of his deeds.*
>
> —JER. 17:10

We are often deceived about our sin, but God is not. He knows whose sin remains unconfessed. He knows who has put up an external façade. His judgment is never predicated on outward appearance or profession, but always on truth. He "sees not as man sees, for man looks at the outward appearance, but the LORD looks at the heart" (1 Sam. 16:7). Is this the omniscient God you know?

FINDING GOD'S WISDOM

God's wisdom could be defined as omniscience acting with a holy will. Tozer explained it this way:

> Wisdom, among other things, is the ability to devise perfect ends and to achieve those ends by the most perfect means. It sees the end from the beginning, so there can be no need to guess or conjecture. Wisdom sees everything in focus, each in proper relation to all, and is thus able to work toward predestined goals with flawless precision.
>
> All God's acts are done in perfect wisdom, first for His own glory, and then for the highest good of the greatest number for the longest time. And all His acts are as pure as they are wise, and as good as they are wise and pure. Not only could His acts not be better done: a better way to do them could not be imagined. (*The Knowledge of the Holy*, p. 66)

God knows the beginning, the end, and every step in between. His perfect knowledge results in perfect wisdom, for He is "the only wise God" (Rom. 16:27).

Unredeemed man, however, views the wisdom of God as foolishness. Paul wrote:

The word of the cross is foolishness to those who are perishing, but to us who are being saved it is the power of God. For it is written, "I will destroy the wisdom of the wise, and the cleverness of the clever I will set aside."

Where is the wise man? Where is the scribe? Where is the debater of this age? Has not God made foolish the wisdom of the world? For since in the wisdom of God *the world through its wisdom did not come to know God, God was well pleased through the foolishness of the message preached to save those who believe. . . .*

We preach Christ crucified, to Jews a stumbling block and to Gentiles foolishness, but to those who are the called, both Jews and Greeks, Christ the power of God and the wisdom of God. *Because the foolishness of God is wiser than men, and the weakness of God is stronger than men. . . . By His doing you are in Christ Jesus, who became to us* wisdom from God, *and righteousness and sanctification, and redemption.*

—1 COR. 1:18-21, 23-25, 30,
EMPHASIS ADDED

The problem with human wisdom is that human reason alone cannot deduce spiritual answers. Human wisdom is defective because human sinfulness has tainted it and because it is unable to perceive the things of God apart from divine revelation (1 Cor. 2:8-14).

God is the only true diagnostician of our condition. That's why David said to Solomon, "Know the God of your father, and serve Him with a whole heart and a willing mind; for the LORD searches all hearts, and understands every intent of the thoughts" (1 Chron. 28:9). God knows everything we do and why we do it. Since He knows everything about the human heart and is able to diagnose its true sinful condition, the solution to that condition is also bound up in His wisdom.

Before the world began, God in His infinite wisdom devised

a plan of redemption so that unworthy sinners might enjoy eternal glory. Paul spoke of this divine wisdom as "a mystery, the hidden wisdom which God predestined before the ages to our glory" (1 Cor. 2:7). It is the Gospel of Christ, "in whom are hidden all the treasures of wisdom and knowledge" (Col. 2:3). Only those who trust in Christ as Savior and Lord possess this wisdom from God.

Paul also said it was his ministry "to bring to light . . . the mystery which for ages has been hidden in God . . . so that *the manifold wisdom of God* might now be made known through the church to the rulers and the authorities in the heavenly places" (Eph. 3:9-10, emphasis added). The Greek word for "manifold" is found only here in the New Testament and means "multicolored." Sinclair Ferguson wrote, "God's wisdom is like the rainbow, in symmetry, beauty, and variety. He does not paint scenes merely in black and white, but uses a riot of colour from the heavenly palette in order to show the wonder of His wise dealings with His people" (*A Heart for God* [Carlisle, Penn.: The Banner of Truth Trust, 1987], p. 72).

This multicolored wisdom of God is put on display before angels "through the church" (Eph. 3:10). The angels can see the power of God in creation, the wrath of God at Mount Sinai, and the love of God at Calvary. But they see the wisdom of God in the church.

It was God's wise and eternal plan to take Jew and Gentile, male and female, slave and free and make them one with the Father, the Son, and the Holy Spirit. In light of that, Paul exclaimed, "Oh, the depth of the riches both of the wisdom and knowledge of God! How unsearchable are His judgments and unfathomable His ways!" (Rom. 11:33).

CONFIDENCE AMIDST DIFFICULTY

When I was a child, the doctrine of omniscience was anything but confidence-inspiring to me. My parents were quick to remind me that God knew everything I did. But as I grew up, I began to realize that God's omniscience is truly a benefit for the Christian.

God's omniscience certainly proved beneficial for Peter, as revealed in this conversation he had with Christ:

Jesus said to Simon Peter, "Simon, son of John, do you love Me . . . ?"

He said to Him, "Yes, Lord; You know that I love You."

He said to him, "Tend My lambs."

He said to him again a second time, "Simon, son of John, do you love Me?"

He said to Him, "Yes, Lord; You know that I love You."

He said to him, "Shepherd My sheep."

He said to him the third time, "Simon, son of John, do you love Me?"

Peter was grieved because He said to him the third time, "Do you love Me?" And he said to Him, "Lord, You know all things; You know that I love You."

Jesus said to him, "Tend My sheep. Truly, truly, I say to you, when you were younger, you used to gird yourself and walk wherever you wished; but when you grow old, you will stretch out your hands and someone else will gird you, and bring you where you do not wish to go."

Now this He said, signifying by what kind of death he would glorify God. And when He had spoken this, He said to him, "Follow Me!"

—JOHN 21:15-19,
EMPHASIS ADDED

After trying twice to convince Christ that he loved Him, Peter then appealed to Christ's omniscience. Peter had previously denied Him three times, but he was nevertheless confident that the all-knowing God knew what was really in his heart. Because Christ did indeed know of Peter's love, He told him to minister to His believers.

Christ knew not only what was in Peter's heart, but also how Peter would die. From what we see of Peter in the rest of the New Testament, that prospect of persecution and death didn't cause him to waver one bit. In the book of Acts we see his courage and confidence in proclaiming the gospel message. After being released from prison and ordered not to evangelize, Peter boldly stated for all time, "We must obey God rather than men" (Acts 5:29).

Where did he get such confidence? The Holy Spirit had certainly empowered him. But undoubtedly there was another underlying reason: He was convinced that God knew what was best for his life. He was willing to place his trust in the God whose wisdom is perfect and whose knowledge is infinite.

What about you? Is that how you know God? Are you willing to trust Him unreservedly with your life?

COMFORT FOR EVERY SITUATION

Have you ever wondered whether God has forgotten you? That's how a small group of godly people in the days of Malachi felt. They lived in the midst of a corrupt and wicked society, and they became fearful, questioning in essence, "When God judges the wicked, will He forget that we belong to Him and judge us along with them?" In Malachi 3:16-17 we read:

> Those who feared the LORD spoke to one another, and the LORD gave attention and heard it, and a book of remembrance was written before Him for those who fear the LORD and who esteem His name. "They will be Mine," says the

LORD *of hosts, "on the day that I prepare My own posses-*
sion, and I will spare them as a man spares his own son who
serves him."

God knew of their devotion to Him. He even recorded it in
a book—not because He forgets, but because He wanted to provide comfort and assurance for those precious believers. God
knows all who belong to Him, for He put their names in the
Book of Life before the world began (Eph. 1:4).

Like the believers in Malachi's day, David too found comfort in God's omniscience. He was aware that God was intimately acquainted with all his ways, for he said, "You have
taken account of my wanderings; put my tears in Your bottle" (Ps. 56:8). It was a common practice in the Orient to
hire mourners for funerals. Those mourners would catch
their tears in a bottle. Perhaps that was how they proved
they had earned their salary. David's statement that God
catches our tears tells us He knows why we have them. His
knowledge of us is intimate, for He knows every trial we
must endure.

That great reality comforted a minister who lived during one
of the stormiest periods of English history. His name was
Richard Baxter, and he was an adviser to Lord Protector Oliver
Cromwell during the English civil war (in the seventeenth century). Because of his Puritan beliefs, Baxter later was persecuted,
imprisoned, and forbidden to preach.

At seventy years of age and suffering from tuberculosis, he
was sentenced to eighteen months in prison. Although Baxter's
circumstances were bleak, this poem of his reflects his unfailing
faith in our all-knowing God and Savior:

> *Lord, it belongs not to my care*
> *Whether I die or live;*
> *To love and serve Thee is my share,*
> *And this Thy grace must give.*

If life be long, I will be glad,
That I may long obey;
If short, yet why should I be sad
To welcome endless day?

Christ leads me through no darker rooms
Than He went through before;
He that into God's kingdom comes
Must enter by this door.

Come, Lord, when grace hath made me meet
Thy blessed face to see;
For if Thy work on earth be sweet,
What will Thy glory be?

My knowledge of that life is small,
The eye of faith is dim;
But 'tis enough that Christ knows all,
And I shall be with Him.

Richard Baxter clung to the Lord's omniscience, and you can too.

5

OUR OMNIPRESENT GOD

During World War II my friend Herb Clingen, his pregnant wife, and their young son spent three years in a Japanese prison camp at Los Baños, in the Philippines, where they had been serving as missionaries. Years later they wrote:

> We did not know it, but our captors expected American soldiers to attempt a rescue at any time. The camp guards were prepared for a wholesale massacre. They had positioned large drums of gasoline throughout the barracks. If American soldiers tried to rescue us, the gasoline would be set ablaze. Prisoners running out of the barracks amid flames and confusion would be cut down with machine-gun fire. . . .
>
> Worse, at the POW camp on Palawan, Japanese guards, mistakenly thinking they were going to be attacked, had forced 140 prisoners into underground shelters, doused them with gasoline, and set them ablaze. Los Baños was set for a similar holocaust, only this time with civilians—including hundreds of women and children. (Herb and Ruth Clingen, "Song of Deliverance," *Masterpiece* magazine, Spring 1989, p. 10)

Herb kept a diary while imprisoned. In one entry he recorded this:

> The situation at present: one death per day for the last six or seven days. These caused by malnutrition resulting in beriberi.

Our only hope is God. Never before have I been so thrown upon the Lord. It won't be long now. . . . The prayer of my heart is that I shall not fail Him. "Be anxious for nothing" (Philippians 4:6). "Though He slay me yet will I trust Him." (Ibid., p. 12)

The very day they were scheduled to be exterminated, however, General Douglas MacArthur and his forces liberated them from captivity. Although they were in great danger, Herb and Ruth found great comfort in God's abiding presence.

It's reassuring to know that God is with His beloved children wherever they are—especially if they are facing death in a prison camp thousands of miles from home! How sad, though, that throughout history people have tried to limit the presence of God. The people of Israel, for example, endeavored to confine Him to the temple in Jerusalem. Many believed He dwelt in that actual building. God, however, cannot be limited to a structure built by human hands.

The *Shekinah* did dwell between the wings of the cherubim at the top of the mercy seat; but it was only a symbol of God's presence, not the full essence of it. Solomon understood that truth, for in dedicating the temple to the Lord, he prayed, "Will God indeed dwell on the earth? Behold, heaven and the highest heaven cannot contain You, how much less this house which I have built!" (1 Kings 8:27). God was present at the temple, but He was also present everywhere else. An understanding Jewish person knew that the temple was but a reminder of God's omnipresence.

In the Old Testament, the tabernacle and the temple were actual locations where God symbolically established the throne of His majesty. Today the church, which is made up of believers, represents the throne of God. In the millennial kingdom, Christ, ruling on the throne of David in Jerusalem, will represent the presence of God. In heaven, the throne (Revelation 4—5) will represent Him. But any symbol of His presence is never the prison of His essence.

As previously noted, the Israelites were not the only ones who tried to confine God's presence. The Syrians, who worshiped the god of the valleys, assumed the God of Israel to be the god of the mountains (1 Kings 20:23). Clearly Mount Sinai, Mount Gerizim, the plateau of Jerusalem, and other such mountains played an important role in the worship of Israel. We know that the prophets often went up into the mountains to pray, as did Christ. But the Creator of all the world cannot be limited to a mountain.

Even today many who call themselves Christians try to limit God. They see Him as a figure confined to heaven, sitting on a brilliant throne way off in some celestial palace. They do not think of Him as being anywhere else.

God, however, could never be confined to any one place because He is omnipresent. His Being fills up endless infinity. God Himself declared, "Do I not fill the heavens and the earth?" (Jer. 23:24). There is no end to Him. He is everywhere. Stephen Charnock wrote:

> As [God] is not measured by time, so He is not limited by place. . . . God, because infinite, fills all, yet so as not to be contained in them, as wine and water is in a vessel. He is from the height of the heaven to the bottom of the deeps, in every point of the world, and in the whole circle of it, yet not limited by it, but beyond it. (*The Existence and Attributes of God* [Minneapolis: Klock & Klock, 1977], p. 148)

His being knows no limits. Samuel Storms in *The Grandeur of God* said:

> God is omnipresent according to His operation. He is not present in creation as a king in his realm or a captain aboard his ship. He does not act upon the world from a distance; but with His whole being He is present powerfully here and everywhere with respect to His essence and power.

Although God is wholly present throughout all things, He is yet distinct from all things. The universe is the creation of God and thus, in respect to essence, no part of Him. So although all things are permeated and sustained by God (Col. 1:16-17; Acts 17:28), God is not all things.

Being wholly spirit, God cannot be divided or separated such that one part of His being is in one place, and another part somewhere else. The whole of His being is always everywhere. (Excerpt from *Masterpiece* magazine, September/October 1989, pp. 8-9)

Now, lest you're beginning to suspect that the omnipresence of God is of interest or relevance only to theologians of previous centuries, there's at least one public official who would disagree with you. Writing in the opinion section of the *Los Angeles Times* on a topic of great interest to Christians in the 1990s, he concluded:

Americans may reasonably differ on whether state-crafted prayer should be authorized in public schools, but it is an insecure, if not manipulative, view of the Christian faith to imply that an agency of the state can block the presence of God. God is not excludable from any place. A U.S. Supreme Court cannot keep an omnipresent God out of our schools any more than Congress is needed to put Him back in. (James A. Leach, "Personal Perspective," September 6, 1992, M-6)

IF GOD IS OMNIPRESENT, WHAT ABOUT . . .

Some argue that if God is everywhere, He must be impure because the impure things that touch Him would defile Him. But that is not so.

As a holy God, He does enter the hearts of sinners to inspect them and convict them of sin. But His essence is never mingled with any impurity. He is like the sun's rays: A sunbeam may fall on a pile of refuse, but that pile cannot defile the sunbeam. Similarly, nothing can defile God. For example, our Lord Jesus

Christ came into the world and lived among sinners. Yet the apostle John said of Him, "In Him there is no sin" (1 John 3:5). He interacted with sinful men and women throughout His life on earth but remained totally undefiled by them.

Another objection some have to the doctrine of God's omnipresence is commonly phrased like this: "Doesn't the Bible say that God is near to some people and far from others? How can He be both near and far when He is everywhere all the time?"

Isaiah did exhort the people to call on the Lord "while He is near" (55:6). Elsewhere he said that Israel's rebellion had caused God to be far from them (29:13; cf. Prov. 15:29). The important thing to keep in mind is the distinction between God's *essence* and His *relation* to people. He is everywhere in His essence, but only in certain places relationally.

In a relational sense, both the Holy Spirit and the Lord Jesus reside in every true believer (Rom. 8:9; Eph. 3:17; Col. 3:11). Paul wrote, "Christ in you, the hope of glory" (Col. 1:27). But before He ever indwelt us relationally as believers, His essence was present to convict us of our sin and save us.

Unbroken Communion with God

As noted in a previous chapter, God is Spirit—He is immaterial and invisible. Therefore, He cannot be reduced to an image or confined to a place. Because of that reality, we can enjoy unbroken communion with God anywhere, not just at a specific time or place.

Even in Old Testament times, worship and communion with God were not limited to a specific time or place. The Jewish people had the temple as a special place of worship, but God's symbolic presence was intended to promote worship *as a way of life.* God deeply desired that their worship of Him would go way beyond the Sabbath and feast days.

Paul, speaking to the philosophers of Athens, said, "The God who made the world and all things in it, since He is Lord of heaven and earth, does not dwell in temples made with hands; nor is He served by human hands, as though He needed anything, since He Himself gives to all people life and breath and all things . . . that they would seek God, if perhaps they might grope for Him and find Him, though He is not far from each one of us" (Acts 17:24-25, 27). The God who extends through all time, space, infinity, and eternity cannot be confined or limited. Therefore, we can commune with Him at all times and in all places.

Jesus made this very important declaration: "Believe Me, an hour is coming when neither in this mountain [Mount Gerizim] nor in Jerusalem will you worship the Father" (John 4:21). What exactly was He saying?

In an individual sense He could have been saying, "You're about to enter into a relationship with God through Me that will enable you to worship God in your heart, not just in a geographical location." In a historical sense He could have been saying, "The time is coming when Jerusalem will be destroyed." In its widest possible interpretation He could have been saying, "I am going to make redemption possible through the cross of Calvary."

Christ then added, "An hour is coming, and now is, when the true worshipers will worship the Father in spirit and truth" (v. 23). That refers to something future, yet also in the present. Basically He was saying, "I'm standing in a transition. The hour is already here (because I'm here) when the Old Covenant will be gone and the New Covenant will be here. In the New Covenant there will be no specific place—no Jerusalem—to worship in."

Jesus was foretelling the end of the Jewish ceremonial system of worship. Its end came with His death on the cross. The veil of the temple was then torn in two from top to bottom, exposing the holy of holies (Matt. 27:51). The Spirit of God, the initiator of true worship, took residence in a new temple: the body of the believer (1 Cor. 6:19).

How does that apply to you? Know that you can commune

with God wherever you go. You can commune with Him at the beach, in the mountains, in the country, or in your living room. You can commune with Him while you're driving down the road, sitting under a tree, walking in the woods, sitting on your porch, looking at the stars, or smelling fresh flowers in the morning. A believer can commune with God anywhere because he or she is a living, breathing temple in whom God dwells. The sphere of our communion with Him is unlimited because God is everywhere at all times!

What about you? Is your communion with God restricted to a certain place and time? Or do you enjoy fellowship with Him as a way of life?

John Owen, in his book *Communion with God*, wrote:

> It is an honour to stand in the presence of princes, even if it be as a servant. What honour, then, have all the saints, to stand with boldness in the presence of the Father and there to enjoy His love! What a blessing did the Queen of Sheba pronounce on the servants of Solomon who stood before him and heard his wisdom. But how much more blessed are they who stand continually before the God of Solomon, hearing His wisdom and enjoying His love! (Edited by R. J. K. Law [Carlisle, Penn.: The Banner of Truth Trust, 1991], pp. 34-37)

GOD'S ABIDING PRESENCE

It's especially comforting to know that whatever trials you have to endure, God is always present. It may not always *feel* as if He is, but in reality He is always there. God's promise to His children is: "I will never desert you, nor will I ever forsake you" (Heb. 13:5; cf. Deut. 31:6). David realized that truth, for he wrote:

> *Where can I go from Your Spirit?*
> *Or where can I flee from Your presence?*
> *If I ascend to heaven, You are there;*
> *If I make my bed in Sheol, behold, You are there.*

> *If I take the wings of the dawn,*
> *If I dwell in the remotest part of the sea,*
> *Even there Your hand will lead me.*
>   —Ps. 139:7-10

No one can be separated from the presence of God, and a believer cannot be separated from a relationship with God.

God's abiding presence brought great comfort to Moses. Although God had called him to proclaim His message and lead Israel out of bondage, Moses protested, claiming he lacked the ability to speak to the people. God responded, "I, even I, will be with your mouth, and teach you what you are to say" (Exod. 4:12). That's a practical aspect of God's presence. He is present in support of our service.

That kind of support is evident in the Great Commission, for Jesus said to His disciples, "Go therefore and make disciples of all the nations . . . teaching them to observe all that I commanded you; and lo, I am with you always, even to the end of the age" (Matt. 28:19-20). The Greek word for "lo" is an exclamation to gain attention, and the word "I" is emphatic. The sense of the verse is this: "I, even I, the risen Son of God, am with you always." Be comforted, knowing you ever remain in Christ's presence.

Christ's abiding presence is what makes the task of reaching the world possible. He provides not only all the right instruction but also the power of His own presence. Believers often doubt they have the power to witness for Christ. Instead, they want their pastor to witness for them. But the people have the same resource as the pastor. The power of God is present for *all* His people.

PURSUING GODLINESS

God gives us this reassuring promise: "No temptation has overtaken you but such as is common to man; and God is faithful, who will not allow you to be tempted beyond what you are able, but with the temptation will provide the way of escape also, so that you will be able to endure it" (1 Cor. 10:13). Whenever temptation comes, know that you have the God-given strength to resist it. Although all of us as believers are at different levels of maturity, God meets every individual at his or her level in order to defend and strengthen him or her against temptation.

Knowing that God is always present is a powerful motivation to resist temptation. It makes us realize that everything we do, we do in His presence. When we sin—whether a sin of thought, word, or action—it is done in the presence of God. That was obviously the attitude Joseph had. In refusing to yield to temptation, he said, "How then could I do this great evil and sin against God?" (Gen. 39:9).

For the most part, people prefer to sin when someone isn't watching. We may not be so careful around our family or closest friends because they're already aware of our problems. Aside from them, however, we become quickly embarrassed when we're caught. But realize this: Whenever you sin, it's as if you've ascended to the throne room of God, walked up to the foot of His throne, and sinned right there. Whatever you do, you do in the presence of God. Now that's a sobering thought!

Job said of God, "Does He not see my ways?" (Job 31:4). That was the basis of his integrity (vv. 1-3). "In *all* your ways acknowledge Him," said Solomon (Prov. 3:6, emphasis added). In everything you do, realize that God is always present. That kind of accountability will help direct you and keep you on the right way.

An awareness of God's presence will not only help you flee from sin, but also to endure suffering. Peter said to believers undergoing severe persecution: "This finds favor, if for the sake of conscience toward God a man bears up under sorrows when suffering unjustly" (1 Pet. 2:19). "Conscience toward God" refers to a general awareness of God's presence, which is an incentive for godly conduct. We are to maintain a good testimony before the lost by enduring mistreatment, confident that God is watching over us and is sovereignly controlling every situation. Godly living is a matter of living in the light of God's presence.

Samuel Storms wrote, "God's omnipresence should console the righteous. No matter what the trial, no matter the place of its occurrence, no matter the swiftness with which it assaults, no matter the depth of its power, *God is ever with us!* 'Even though I walk through the valley of the shadow of death, I fear no evil; *for Thou art with me*'" (Ps. 23:4, emphasis added; *Masterpiece*, September/October 1989, p. 9)

THE LORD IS NEAR

Paul wrote, "The Lord is near. Be anxious for nothing" (Phil. 4:5-6). That refers not to Christ's Second Coming, but to His present comforting ministry to us. He is present all the time. The psalmist echoed that truth, saying, "You are near, O LORD" (Ps. 119:151).

The Lord encompasses us with His presence. When you have a thought, the Lord is near to read it; when you pray, He is near to hear it; when you need His strength and power, He is near to provide it.

Such an awareness will help keep you from being anxious. That is a lesson the prophet Habakkuk learned. In his day strife and injustice filled the land. Since he wanted to know why God wasn't doing anything about it, he said:

> *How long, O LORD, will I call for help,*
> *And You will not hear?*
> *I cry out to You, "Violence!"*
> *Yet You do not save.*
>
> —HAB. 1:2

God responded by saying:

Look among the nations! Observe! Be astonished! Wonder! Because I am doing something in your days—You would not believe if you were told. For behold, I am raising up the Chaldeans, that fierce and impetuous people who march throughout the earth to seize dwelling places which are not theirs.

—vv. 5-6

God planned to use a pagan nation to punish Habakkuk's people. That was not the kind of answer the prophet expected to hear. He had a visceral response to the news: "I heard and my inward parts trembled, at the sound my lips quivered. Decay enters my bones, and in my place I tremble. Because I must wait quietly for the day of distress, for the people to arise who will invade us" (3:16).

But then Habakkuk began to remember what he knew about the Lord, and he said, "Are You not from everlasting, O LORD, my God, my Holy One? We will not die" (1:12). Habakkuk reminded himself that the everlasting God was near. Being eternal, God is before, after, above, and independent of history, reigning in eternal timelessness. That truth helped Habakkuk realize that everything is a part of God's eternal plan, including strife and injustice in the land. Invasion by enemy forces would not escape God's notice. It was not an accident. God was near and was sovereignly controlling every circumstance.

Habakkuk reminded himself that the Holy One was near. Remembering that God is perfect and must deal with sin, he acknowledged, "Your eyes are too pure to approve evil, and You can not look on wickedness with favor" (v. 13). He was saying, "I know that God can't act apart from His holiness. Since He is punishing us because of our sin, I know He'll punish the Chaldeans because of their sin too." God was not in a remote place. His holy eyes were present to execute judgment.

Habakkuk then reminded himself of another truth about

God: He is faithful. "We will not die" (v. 12) is an affirmation of God's covenant with His people. He is true to His Word. His faithfulness is inseparable from His covenant love, which is an everlasting love. God is not distant toward His own. His faithfulness and love are intimate.

Perhaps Habakkuk was thinking, "Lord, everything I know about You tells me to stop worrying about this problem. I don't understand it, but I don't need to. In fact, my mind is too small to do so, and it was pride that led me to think I could." Habakkuk, by meditating on the Lord's character, learned this valuable principle: "The righteous will live by his faith" (Hab. 2:4; cf. Rom. 1:17; Heb. 10:38). Habakkuk's strong faith in the Lord is evident in his concluding words:

> *Though the fig tree should not blossom*
> *And there be no fruit on the vines,*
> *Though the yield of the olive should fail*
> *And the fields produce no food,*
> *Though the flock should be cut off from the fold*
> *And there be no cattle in the stalls,*
> *Yet I will exult in the LORD,*
> *I will rejoice in the God of my salvation.*
> *The Lord GOD is my strength,*
> *And He has made my feet like hinds' feet,*
> *And makes me walk on my high places.*
> —HAB. 3:17-19

He was saying, "If all the normal things of life I depend on suddenly fall apart, I'll still place my hope in God. He'll give me the ability and confidence to walk along the precipices of life's cliffs." You can have that kind of confidence too. Knowing the Lord is near will help you "be anxious for nothing" (Phil. 4:6). The Lord who is everywhere can truly handle anything you encounter.

6

OUR OMNIPOTENT GOD

In her article "Historic Grab in Space" Marcia Dunn wrote:

> Three spacewalking astronauts reached up with their gloved
> hands yesterday and caught a 41/2-ton, slowly spinning satel-
> lite in a risky, last-ditch attempt to save the craft.
>
> "Houston, I think we got a satellite," said shuttle com-
> mander Daniel Brandenstein from inside the *Endeavor* after
> the three astronauts, standing in a circle outside the craft, put
> their hands on the bottom of the satellite and held it steady. . . .
>
> The *Endeavor* had just passed to the southwest of Hawaii,
> 225 miles high and traveling at 17,500 [miles] per hour. . . .
> The three astronauts surrounded the satellite like three legs of
> a tripod. The operation required extraordinary delicacy; any
> jarring motion could have caused the fuel inside the satellite
> to start it rocking.
>
> The shuttle was in a tail-to-Earth position, and the planet's
> mottled blue globe turned slowly behind the astronauts as
> they captured the satellite. (*San Francisco Chronicle*, May 14,
> 1992, pp. 1, 5)

Certainly that was a historic grab in space. The ability to
launch into space and catch by hand a satellite weighing much
more than an elephant should amaze us all. But as astonishing
as that is, it is insignificant compared to the ability of God.

God is omnipotent. He has the ability and power to do

anything. Even one of the Hebrew names for God, *El Shaddai*, speaks of His power. *El* speaks of God, and *Shaddai* means "almighty." That name refers to His awesome strength and might. Job said, "If it is a matter of power, behold, He is the strong one!" (Job 9:19). He realized that absolute strength and might belong to God alone. The apostle John exclaimed, "Alleluia: for the Lord God omnipotent reigneth" (Rev. 19:6, KJV).

Isaiah said of God's awesome power, "Behold, the nations are like a drop from a bucket, and are regarded as a speck of dust on the scales; behold, He lifts up the islands like fine dust. Even Lebanon is not enough to burn, nor its beasts enough for a burnt offering. All the nations are as nothing before Him, they are regarded by Him as less than nothing and meaningless" (40:15-17).

When God exercises His power, He does so effortlessly. It is no more difficult for Him to create a universe than to make a butterfly. A. W. Tozer wrote:

> Since He has at His command all the power in the universe, the Lord God omnipotent can do anything as easily as anything else. All His acts are done without effort. He expends no energy that must be replenished. His self-sufficiency makes it unnecessary for Him to look outside of Himself for a renewal of strength. All the power required to do all that He wills to do lies in undiminished fullness in His own infinite being. (*The Knowledge of the Holy* [New York: Harper & Row, 1961], p. 73)

Stephen Charnock expands our thinking on that topic:

> The omnipotence of God is His ability and strength to bring to pass whatsoever He pleases.
>
> Our desires may be—and are—more extensive than our power, but with God, "His counsel shall stand, and He will do all His pleasure" (Isa. 46:10). You must, in your concep-

tion of divine power, enlarge it further than to think God can do only what He resolves to do. In truth He has as infinite a capacity of power to act as He has an infinite capacity of will to resolve. His power is such that He can do whatever He pleases without difficulty or resistance; He cannot be checked, restrained, or frustrated.

How worthless His eternal counsels would be if His power could not execute them. His mercy would be a feeble pity if He were destitute of power to relieve, His justice a slighted scarecrow without power to punish, and His promises an empty sound without the strength to accomplish them. (Cited in *Masterpiece* magazine, September/October 1989, p. 10)

Because God's power is infinite, He "does not become weary or tired" (Isa. 40:28).

People often question what God does, but they don't understand that He can do anything He wants. The psalmist said, "Our God is in the heavens; He does whatever He pleases" (Ps. 115:3). Paul illustrated God's sovereignty in showing mercy on some (Isaac and Jacob) while hardening others (Esau and Pharaoh). To the one who argues with God's right to make those distinctions, he stated frankly, "Who are you, O man, who answers back to God? The thing molded will not say to the molder, 'Why did you make me like this,' will it? Or does not the potter have a right over the clay . . . ?" (Rom. 9:20-21).

Although such power might seem frightful, remember that God is good. He can do anything according to His infinite ability, but He will do only those things that are consistent with Himself. That's why He can't lie, tolerate sin, or save impenitent sinners.

THE EXPRESSION OF GOD'S POWER

God's power expresses itself in an infinite number of ways. Let's look at a few.

In Creation

David praised our Creator God, saying, "By the word of the LORD the heavens were made, and by the breath of His mouth all their host" (Ps. 33:6). No one helped God create the world, for He said, "I, the LORD, am the Maker of all things, stretching out the heavens by Myself and spreading out the earth all alone" (Isa. 44:24). He willed creation into existence, calling "into being that which does not exist" (Rom. 4:17). Contemplating His creation should cause us to appreciate His great power. Yet God's power is greater than anything He has ever made.

What God creates He also sustains, maintains, and preserves. He "upholds all things by the word of His power" (Heb. 1:3). The Greek word translated "uphold" means "to support" or "to maintain." It is used in the present tense, implying continuous action. At this moment God is sustaining everything in the universe. That is much more than a law of nature; it is the very activity of God.

Can you imagine what would happen if God were to relinquish His sustaining power? We would cease to exist. Our lives depend on the constancy of the physical laws He has established.

If God were to stop maintaining the law of gravity, we wouldn't be able to stay on the earth and would surely die. Or consider the sun. It has a surface temperature of 12,000 degrees Fahrenheit. If it were closer to the earth, we'd burn; if it were farther, we'd freeze.

Furthermore, our globe is tilted on an exact angle of 23 degrees, which enables us to have four seasons. If it weren't tilted, vapors from the ocean would move north and south, eventually piling up monstrous continents of ice. If our atmosphere suddenly thinned out, the meteors that now harmlessly burn up when they hit it would constantly bombard us on the earth's surface.

If the moon did not remain a specific distance from the

earth, the ocean tides would completely inundate the land twice a day. If the ocean floor merely slipped a few feet deeper, the carbon dioxide and oxygen balance in the earth's atmosphere would be completely upset, and no vegetable or animal life could exist on earth.

Things don't happen in our universe by accident. God sustains it. He is the principle of cohesion. He is not some remote watchmaker who made the world, set it in motion, and hasn't bothered it since. The reason the universe is a cosmos and not chaos—an ordered and reliable system instead of an erratic and unpredictable muddle—is because of the upholding power of God. Scientists who think they are discovering great truths are doing nothing more than discovering the sustaining laws that God uses to control the world. No scientist, mathematician, or astronomer could discover anything apart from the upholding power of God because He monitors and sustains the movements and developments of the entire universe. His governing of the whole cosmos manifests His unsearchable wisdom and boundless power. And He upholds it all "by the word of His power."

A question often raised is: If God never gets tired as He preserves and maintains the universe, why did He rest on the seventh day of Creation? The answer is, God didn't literally rest. He merely finished His work of Creation. If He had rested, everything He had made on the first six days would have fallen apart. God doesn't get tired, and He was just as active on the seventh day as He was on the other six, upholding everything He had made.

In Salvation

F. B. Meyer wrote:

> We go into the artist's studio and find there unfinished pictures covering large canvases, and suggesting great designs, but which have been left, either because the genius was not

competent to complete the work, or because paralysis laid the hand low in death; but as we go into God's great workshop we find nothing that bears the mark of haste or insufficiency of power to finish, and we are sure that the work which His grace has begun, the arm of His strength will complete. (*The Epistle to the Philippians* [Grand Rapids, Mich.: Zondervan, 1952], p. 21)

That was the point Paul made when he said, "He who began a good work in you will perfect it until the day of Christ Jesus" (Phil. 1:6). Salvation is a powerful work of God. When God begins that great work in a person, He inevitably brings it to its conclusion. God always finishes what He starts.

Jude ended his letter on that same note:

Now to Him who is able to keep you from stumbling, and to make you stand in the presence of His glory blameless with great joy, to the only God our Savior, through Jesus Christ our Lord, be glory, majesty, dominion and authority, before all time and now and forever. Amen.

—vv. 24-25

Salvation isn't like my experience playing football. I remember going into the locker room after a game and hearing the coach say, "Hey, you're the reason we lost the game. Not only did you fumble the ball on the three-yard line, but you let the guy from the other team pick it up and run for a touchdown. It was your fault! Next time hold onto the ball!"

No fault-finding will occur in heaven. The Lord will never say to any believer, "Do you realize that because of what you did, 200 people didn't get here?" Salvation means that the Lord carries all repentant sinners from justification to glorification (Rom. 8:30). He will never fail to bring in all the elect, because He is the all-powerful God.

Redemption was an even greater display of God's power

than Creation. There apparently was no opposition to Creation, but in redemption the devil had to be subdued, death had to be conquered, and sin had to be dealt with. God then chose "the weak things of the world to shame the things which are strong" (1 Cor. 1:27). God sent common people out into the world to spread the good news of salvation. And within a short time they turned the world upside-down (Acts 17:6).

In the Resurrection

God's power is also manifested in His ability to raise the dead. Jesus said to His disciples, "After I have been raised, I will go ahead of you to Galilee" (Matt. 26:32).

The Jewish people as a whole rejected the messianic claims of Christ. He was accused of being an insurrectionist who was involved in revolutionary activities aimed at overthrowing the Roman government. The religious leaders brought Him before Pilate, the governor, claiming that He was a threat not only to Judaism but to the Roman political system as well.

Their political accusations against Christ were untrue: He did not set Himself against Rome. However, their religious accusations were true: Christ did claim to be the Messiah (Mark 14:61-62). He knew that His true confession of deity would cost Him His life, but He never equivocated His message, even in the face of imminent danger and death. Christ confessed openly His lordship, messianic identity, and sovereign authority. Why? Because He committed His life to the One who is able to raise the dead. And, indeed, He "was raised from the dead through the glory of the Father" (Rom. 6:4).

Christ was able to face the cross not only because of the Father's power, but also because of His own. He Himself had the power to conquer death. Jesus said, "I lay down My life that I may take it again. No one has taken it away from Me, but I lay it down on My own initiative. I have authority to lay it down, and I have authority to take it up again" (John 10:17-18).

Through His death He rendered powerless the devil, who had "the power of death" (Heb. 2:14). He took on death as an enemy and won hands down.

God has so much power that at the end of the age He will raise from the dead every human being who has ever lived—both the righteous and unrighteous. "An hour is coming," Jesus said, "in which all who are in the tombs shall hear His [God's] voice, and will come forth; those who did the good deeds, to a resurrection of life, those who committed the evil deeds to a resurrection of judgment" (John 5:28-29). In addition, the book of Revelation refers to the Great White Throne Judgment, where all the ungodly will be brought before God (Rev. 20:11-15).

THE GREATNESS OF GOD'S POWER

Paul wrote, "I pray that the eyes of your *heart* may be enlightened, so that you will know . . . what is the surpassing greatness of His power toward us who believe . . . in accordance with the working of the strength of His might" (Eph. 1:18-19, emphasis added). The great truths of a believer's position in Christ are profound and difficult for the human mind to grasp, but not impossibly so.

Many people misunderstand the meaning of *heart* in Scripture because Western culture often uses the term to refer to our emotions. Many of our love songs refer to the heart. But the term as used in Scripture refers to the thinking processes—the mind, will, and understanding (cf. Prov. 23:7, KJV). The mind is the instrument of spiritual perception and understanding.

What are we to understand about God's power? That it is the source of *our* spiritual power. In Ephesians 1:19 Paul used four different words to describe the power that God gives to us. The first is *dunamis*, from which we derive the English word *dynamite*. It is translated "power" and refers to inherent power. The second is *energeia*, from which we derive the English word *energy*. It is translated "working" and refers to operative power.

The third is *kratos*. It can be translated "strength" or "dominion" and refers to ultimate power. The fourth is *ischus*. It is translated "might" and refers to endowed power. God has given us incredible power. Many times you might find yourself saying you don't have enough power or strength to handle a situation, but that's not really true. God's great power is available and sufficient for your every need (Phil. 4:13, 19).

APPLYING GOD'S POWER

How does God's power apply to our lives as believers? Here are a few ways.

For Worship

We are to worship God because of His power. God said to His people, "The LORD, who brought you up from the land of Egypt with great power and with an outstretched arm, Him you shall fear, and to Him you shall bow yourselves down" (2 Kings 17:36). That applies as much to His people today as it did to the Israelites then. We ought to meditate more on His power. Doing so will help us focus less on our problems.

For Confidence

God's power is a source of confidence. Whenever you feel inadequate, remember Paul's words: "I can do all things through Him who strengthens me" (Phil. 4:13). In the strength of God's power we can accomplish all that He calls us to do (1 Thess. 5:24). We can live confidently every day, knowing that we are "able to do exceeding abundantly beyond all that we ask or think, according to the power that works within us" (Eph. 3:20).

For Hope

God's resurrection power is the basis of our hope. Paul's testimony was this:

*For to me, to live is Christ and to die is gain. But if I am to live
on in the flesh, this will mean fruitful labor for me; and I do
not know which to choose. But I am hard-pressed from both
directions, having the desire to depart and be with Christ, for
that is very much better; yet to remain on in the flesh is more
necessary for your sake.*

—PHIL. 1:21-24

Paul didn't know all the details of God's specific plan for his
life, but he was confident in it, whether it meant life or death.
He preferred the joy of being in Christ's presence in heaven, but
apparently he thought God would let him live because he knew
the Philippians needed him.

Since Christ was Paul's whole life, dying could only be a gain
since it would usher him into the Lord's presence. His confidence
in the Lord's ability to raise the dead helped him not be intimidated by suffering or death. He could devote himself fully to the
Lord, not forsaking his spiritual duty to preserve his own life.
The hope of the resurrection should help us have priorities that
are eternal, not temporal, as well.

The resurrection power of God was no mystery to Old
Testament believers. Job said, "I know that my Redeemer lives,
and at the last He will take His stand on the earth. Even after
my skin is destroyed, yet from my flesh I shall see God; whom I
myself shall behold, and whom my eyes will see and not
another" (Job 19:25-27). Knowing that the Lord is all-powerful helped him endure great suffering.

Daniel also knew of God's resurrection power, for an angel
said to him, "Many of those who sleep in the dust of the ground
will awake, these to everlasting life, but the others to disgrace and
everlasting contempt" (Dan. 12:2). The resurrection to everlasting life is a resurrection of the just (Acts 24:15). All true believers
will enjoy eternal life. The resurrection to disgrace and everlasting contempt will happen at the end of the Millennium, when God
raises the bodies of the unjust from the dead (cf. Rev. 20:11-15).

Isaiah, who lived more than a century before Daniel, predicted that the dead would live again:

> *Your dead will live;*
> *Their corpses will rise.*
> *You who lie in the dust, awake*
> *and shout for joy,*
> *For . . . the earth will give birth to*
> *the departed spirits.*
>
> —26:19

The Lord through Hosea, a contemporary of Isaiah, said:

> *Shall I ransom them from the power of Sheol?*
> *Shall I redeem them from death?*
> *O Death, where are your thorns?*
> *O Sheol, where is your sting?*
>
> —13:14

David wrote:

> *My heart is glad and my glory rejoices;*
> *My flesh also will dwell securely.*
> *For You will not abandon my soul to Sheol;*
> *Nor will You allow Your Holy One [Christ]*
> *to undergo decay.*
>
> —Ps. 16:9-10

Thinking of God's resurrection power should likewise fill our hearts with joy, "knowing that He who raised the Lord Jesus will raise us also" (2 Cor. 4:14).

For Comfort

When you catch yourself worrying about something, realize anew that there is nothing too great for God to handle. God Himself says to you, "Behold, I am the LORD, the God of all flesh; is anything too difficult for Me?" (Jer. 32:27). Nothing is impossible for Him because His power is infinite. A. W. Pink wrote:

> Well may the saint trust such a God! He is worthy of implicit confidence. Nothing is too hard for Him. If God were stinted in might and had a limit to His strength we might well despair. But seeing that He is clothed with omnipotence, no prayer is too hard for Him to answer, no need too great for Him to supply, no passion too strong for Him to subdue; no temptation too powerful for Him to deliver from, no misery too deep for Him to relieve. (*The Attributes of God* [Grand Rapids, Mich.: Baker, 1975], p. 51)

Stephen Charnock adds this reassuring thought:

> As omnipotence is an ocean that cannot be fathomed, so the comforts from it are streams that cannot be exhausted. How comforting to know you have a God who can do what He pleases: there is nothing so difficult that He can't accomplish, nothing so strong that He can't overrule! You need not dread men since you have One to restrain them, nor fear devils since you have One to chain them. His power was not all expended in creation; it is not weakened by His preservation of all things. For whom would the Lord display His eternal arm and the incomprehensible thunder of His power but for His own? (Cited in *Masterpiece* magazine, September/October 1987, p. 10)

God can handle any problem you have!

For Victory

God's power is the basis for our spiritual victory. Paul tells us to "be strong in the Lord and in the strength of His might" (Eph. 6:10). To experience victory, you must be like a guard on watch. When the enemy comes, you're not supposed to fight him yourself—you are to tell the commander, and he will lead the battle. God can bring about spiritual victory because "greater is He who is in you than he who is in the world" (1 John 4:4). Satan is a powerful enemy, but he is no match for God's power.

What should be our response to God's awesome, majestic, and glorious power? Humility. It's easy to be proud if your thoughts are on yourself instead of God. That's why we need to heed this admonition: "Humble yourselves under the mighty hand of God, that He may exalt you at the proper time" (1 Pet. 5:6). We need to humble ourselves before our all-powerful God because apart from His enabling, we can do nothing (Deut. 8:18; John 15:5; 2 Cor. 3:5).

THE WRATH OF OUR GOD

On July 8, 1741, Jonathan Edwards preached the most famous sermon in American history. That sermon, "Sinners in the Hands of an Angry God," presents the true condition of fallen humanity and the need for salvation. Here is an excerpt from his message:

> Your wickedness makes you as it were heavy as lead, and to tend downwards with great weight and pressure towards hell; and if God should let you go, you would immediately sink and swiftly descend and plunge into the bottomless gulf, and your healthy constitution, and your own care and prudence, and best contrivance, and all your righteousness, would have no more influence to uphold you and keep you out of hell, than a spider's web would have to stop a falling rock. . . .
>
> There are the black clouds of God's wrath now hanging directly over your heads, full of the dreadful storm, and big with thunder; and were it not for the restraining hand of God, it would immediately burst forth upon you. The sovereign pleasure of God, for the present, stays his rough wind; otherwise it would come with fury, and your destruction would come like a whirlwind, and you would be like the chaff of the summer threshing floor. ([Phillipsburg, N.J.: Presbyterian and Reformed Publishing, 1992], pp. 20-21)

Most people have an aversion to seeing God as a God of wrath. But that is one of the ways Scripture characterizes Him.

"A jealous and avenging God is the LORD . . .," wrote Nahum the prophet. "The LORD takes vengeance on His adversaries, and He reserves wrath for His enemies. The LORD is slow to anger and great in power, and the LORD will by no means leave the guilty unpunished. . . . Who can stand before His indignation? Who can endure the burning of His anger? His wrath is poured out like fire" (Nahum 1:2-3, 6).

Isaiah said, "Behold, the day of the LORD is coming, cruel, with fury and burning anger, to make the land a desolation; and He will exterminate its sinners from it" (13:9). The Lord Himself said, "Behold, My anger and My wrath will be poured out on this place, on man and on beast and on the trees of the field and on the fruit of the ground; and it will burn and not be quenched" (Jer. 7:20).

In the New Testament John the Baptist declared, "His [God's] winnowing fork is in His hand, and He will thoroughly clean His threshing floor; and He will gather His wheat into the barn, but He will burn up the chaff with unquenchable fire" (Matt. 3:12). Paul said regarding the lost, "Because of your stubbornness and unrepentant heart you are storing up wrath for yourself in the day of wrath and revelation of the righteous judgment of God" (Rom. 2:5). In the book of Revelation we read of Christ, "From His mouth comes a sharp sword, so that with it He may strike down the nations, and He will rule them with a rod of iron; and He treads the wine press of the fierce wrath of God, the Almighty" (19:15).

Scripture paints an absolutely fearful and horrifying picture of God's wrath. Yet today's church has soft-pedaled the theme of judgment and quietly omitted or altered the doctrine of hell. Perhaps you think I am speaking only of liberal churches who deny the inspiration of Scripture and the reality of hell altogether. Sad to say, I am not. A growing trend among evangelicals is annihilationism, the theological doctrine that the wicked will cease to exist after this life (e.g., Edward William Fudge, *The Fire That*

Consumes [Houston: Providential Press, 1982], endorsed by F. F. Bruce, Clark Pinnock, and John Wenham; see also "John Stott on Hell," World Christian [May 1989], pp. 31-37). That doctrine is opposed to the biblical teaching of eternal, conscious torment in hell (e.g., Matt. 25:46; Mark 9:44, 46, 48; Luke 12:47-48; John 5:25-29; Heb. 10:29; Rev. 20:10-15). This is an admittedly emotional issue. One of the evangelical leaders concerned confesses, "I find the concept [of eternal punishment] intolerable and do not understand how people can live with it" (Stott, p. 32).

This is a serious matter because people cannot fully understand God's love without also understanding the extent of His wrath. God is perfect in love—and equally perfect in wrath. Both the Old and New Testaments reflect that balance, saying of God, "You have loved righteousness and hated wickedness" (Ps. 45:7; Heb. 1:9). R. A. Torrey wrote:

> Shallow views of sin and of God's holiness, and of the glory of Jesus Christ and His claims upon us, lie at the bottom of weak theories of the doom of the impenitent. When we see sin in all its hideousness and enormity, the holiness of God in all its perfection, and the glory of Jesus Christ in all its infinity, nothing but a doctrine that those who persist in the choice of sin, who love darkness rather than light, and who persist in the rejection of the Son of God, shall endure everlasting anguish, will satisfy the demands of our own moral intuitions. . . . The more closely men walk with God and the more devoted they become to His service, the more likely they are to believe this doctrine. (What the Bible Teaches [New York: Revell, 1898], pp. 311-313)

THE PURITY OF GOD'S WRATH

The wrath of God is not like human wrath. Most often when we get angry, we are offended and our pride gets in the way. That is a reflection of the evil heart of man. Even when we are angry about the right things, our own sinfulness usually pollutes our anger. That's why we must not impose our concept of anger onto God. God's anger is pure and untainted by sin.

God's wrath is pure because it is related to His holiness, which demands that He not tolerate sin. Christ's cleansing of the temple was a demonstration of His holy wrath (John 2:13-16). That dramatic scene was His first public act in Jerusalem. He made a whip, drove out the people and animals, and overturned the tables because God's name was being dishonored.

God's wrath is also pure because it is related to His justice. Remember what happened to Achan? God told the people of Israel not to steal anything from Jericho, but Achan disobeyed and hid some stolen goods under his tent. Joshua, finding that Achan was guilty, said to him, "My son, I implore you, give glory to the LORD, the God of Israel, and give praise to Him; and tell me now what you have done. Do not hide it from me" (Josh. 7:19).

Why did Joshua say that? Was he going to let Achan off the hook if he confessed? No. He was saying, "Before you get your due judgment from God, confess your sin and admit your guilt. Confess that God's reaction to your sin is just." What was God's judgment? Achan and his family, who must have participated in the act in some way, were put to death.

God never makes a mistake in exercising His wrath. He doesn't fly off the handle in momentary fury. When He is angry, it is the right expression of His holiness and justice.

THE REVELATION OF GOD'S WRATH

Paul said God's wrath "is revealed from heaven" (Rom. 1:18). The literal rendering is, "is constantly being revealed." God's always revealing His wrath. It has been visible throughout human history.

To begin with, God revealed His wrath in the Garden of Eden. When Adam and Eve sinned, they were thrown out of paradise, the earth was cursed, and death became a terrible reality. That was a forceful lesson to the world that God hates sin.

We also see God's wrath manifested in the Flood, about which He said, "I will blot out man whom I have created from the face of the land, from man to animals to creeping things and to birds of the sky; for I am sorry that I have made them" (Gen. 6:7). God also demonstrated His wrath in such things as the destruction of Sodom and Gomorrah, the curse of the Law upon every transgressor, and the institution of the sacrificial system. Perhaps the greatest demonstration of God's wrath was the suffering and crucifixion of Christ. He hates sin so deeply that He poured out His fury on His own beloved Son as He bore our iniquities.

Perhaps you're thinking, *It seems, however, that many people sin and get away with it. Is God's wrath ever revealed against them?* Ultimately, it will be. Jonathan Edwards illustrated that truth this way:

> The wrath of God is like great waters that are dammed for the present; they increase more and more, and rise higher and higher, till an outlet is given; and the longer the stream is stopped, the more rapid and mighty is its course, when once it is let loose.
>
> It is true, that judgment against your evil works has not been executed hitherto; the floods of God's vengeance have been withheld; but your guilt in the mean time is constantly increasing, and you are every day treasuring up more wrath; the waters are constantly rising, and waxing more and more mighty; and there is nothing but the mere pleasure of God, that holds the waters back, that are unwilling to be stopped, and press hard to go forward. If God should only withdraw his hand from the flood-gate, it would immediately fly open, and the fiery floods of the fierceness and wrath of God, would rush forth with inconceivable fury, and would come upon you with omnipotent power. (*Sinners in the Hands of an Angry God*, pp. 21-22)

God may choose to hold back His wrath for a time, but He will ultimately release it with great fury. Paul explained that sinners are stockpiling wrath that will come crashing down on them one day (Rom. 2:5).

David used another analogy to describe how God holds back His wrath: "If a man does not repent, He [God] will sharpen His sword; He has bent His bow and made it ready. He has also prepared for Himself deadly weapons; He makes His arrows fiery shafts" (Ps. 7:12-13). The longer God pulls back the bow, the deeper the arrow will plunge when He releases it.

If it seems that the sins of men and women go unchecked, it may be that God is storing up the waters of His wrath and sharpening His sword. He will settle all accounts in His perfect time and way.

The story is told of a farming community in which most of the farmers were godly men who gathered to worship the Lord on Sunday instead of working their fields. One exception was a farmer who was an atheist. He considered himself a freethinker and often chided his neighbors, saying, "Hands that work are better than hands that pray." Part of his land bordered the church, and he would make a point of driving his tractor by during worship services. When one year his land produced more than anyone else's in the county, he submitted a lengthy letter to the editor of the local paper, boasting of what a man can do on his own without God. The editor printed the man's letter, then added this pithy comment: "God doesn't settle all His accounts in the month of October."

THE PERSONAL NATURE OF GOD'S WRATH

God reveals His wrath from heaven through personal involvement. He is not a cosmic force who made physical and moral laws and just lets them run their course. His wrath is not an automatic judgment by an anonymous celestial computer. The Bible shows within His heart a very intense personal reaction to sin.

Some of the Hebrew terms used in the Old Testament disclose what God's holy reaction to sin is like. *Charah*, for instance, means "to become heated up, to burn up with fury." God's wrath was kindled against Israel for engaging in immoral pagan rites (Num.

25:3). God instructed Moses to execute all the leaders involved so that His "fierce anger" might be turned away from the people.

Another Old Testament term is *charon*, which refers to a burning, fierce wrath. God's anger burned against the Israelites because they quickly turned aside from His commandments and worshiped a molten calf (Exod. 32:12).

Still another term is *qatsaph*, which means "to be bitter." Because of His passionate love for Israel, God used Gentile nations to chastise her. At the same time, however, He was angry because those nations wanted to annihilate her. Because the nations had an evil motive against His own people, they themselves were subject to His fierce anger (Zech. 1:15).

Chemah refers to venom or poison and is frequently associated with jealousy. God said to Israel, "Thus I will judge you like women who commit adultery or shed blood are judged; and I shall bring on you the blood of wrath and jealousy" (Ezek. 16:38). Because the nation had prostituted herself with the neighboring pagan nations, God's wrath would remain heavily upon her until she learned not to violate the love of her Divine Husband—God.

The term *za'am* also tells us what God's holy reaction to sin is like: It pictures someone who is furious. David wrote, "God is a righteous judge, and a God who has indignation every day" (Ps. 7:11). *The King James Version* has a more vivid translation: "God is angry with the wicked every day."

In the New Testament, Paul wrote that "to those who are selfishly ambitious and do not obey the truth, but obey unrighteousness, [God will render] *wrath* and *indignation*. There will be *tribulation* and *distress* for every soul of man who does evil" (Rom. 2:8-9, emphasis added).

The root of the Greek word translated "wrath" means "to rush along," "to be in a hurry," or "to breathe violently." It has been used since the time of Homer to refer to the rage that swells within a person. In Scripture it is used to describe such things as Pharaoh's desire to kill Moses, the rage of the angry crowd who wanted to throw Jesus off a cliff, and the riot in Ephesus. Likewise, God's wrath will burst out like a consuming fire against those who oppose the lordship of Christ.

The Greek term translated "indignation" speaks of a fevered state of fury. At this point, mercy and grace have ended. God's tolerance erupts into a swelling, furious, final display of anger.

The term translated "tribulation" speaks of putting pressure on someone or something. It specifically refers to an affliction that results in personal suffering, such as Christ's sufferings and the crushing persecution endured by the early church.

The word translated "distress" literally means "narrow," referring to the narrowness or confinement of a place. This confinement produces unimaginable discomfort, and it refers to the kind of distress that the ungodly experience in hell. The New Testament describes hell as an everlasting punishment, an everlasting fire, a furnace of fire, a lake of fire, fire and brimstone, an unquenchable fire, and a place of suffering (note the references earlier in this chapter).

THE OBJECT OF GOD'S WRATH

God's wrath is revealed "against all ungodliness and unrighteousness of men" (Rom. 1:18). His wrath is against sin. It's not uncontrolled, irrational fury like that of a criminal who might take his or her vengeance out on the nearest person, but rather it is discriminatingly and carefully pointed at "ungodliness and unrighteousness."

"Ungodliness" is the result of a person's broken relationship with God. God's anger is against those who are not rightly related to Him. The ungodliness of unbelievers is evidenced by their impiety toward God—their lack of reverence, devotion, and worship, which leads to idolatry.

"Unrighteousness" also affects people's relationships with others. If you are not rightly related to God and therefore fail to revere Him, your relationships with everyone else around you will not be right either. Sin first attacks God's majesty and His Law; then it attacks others. People treat one another unrighteously because that's how they treat God. By not being rightly related to God, a person's relationships and transactions become corrupted. "Ungodliness" leads to "unrighteousness"; a failure to honor God's laws leads to the evil treatment of others.

It's no wonder that God hates sin. It's the one thing that will keep any person from entering His presence and from rightly relating to others.

THE REASON FOR GOD'S WRATH

There are many reasons for God's wrath, but let's focus on just one, which is the sin of rejecting God's revelation of Himself in creation. Paul wrote that even though everyone who has ever lived is aware of God's existence, "they did not honor Him as God or give thanks, but they became futile in their speculations, and their foolish heart was darkened" (Rom. 1:21).

Should you ever doubt that everyone starts off with an awareness of God, consider the amazing testimony of Helen Keller. When Helen was an infant, a disease robbed her of the ability to see, hear, or speak. Through the tireless efforts of her tutor, Anne Sullivan, Helen learned to communicate through touch and later even learned to talk. When Miss Sullivan first tried to tell Helen about God, Helen responded that she already knew about Him— she just didn't know His name (Helen Keller, *The Story of My Life* [New York: Grosset & Dunlap, 1905], pp. 368-374).

Creation has provided every man and woman with enough light to perceive God's sustaining power and deity. But we all eventually reject that revelation. In fact, the things God gave people to lead them to Himself became the very things they used to crucify Christ. Donald Grey Barnhouse explained:

> God will give a man brains to smelt iron and make a hammer head and nails. God will grow a tree and give man strength to

cut it down and brains to fashion a hammer handle from its wood. And when man has the hammer and the nails, God will put out His hand and let man drive nails through it and place Him on the cross in the supreme demonstration that men are without excuse. (*Romans*, Vol. 1 [Grand Rapids, Mich.: Eerdmans, 1953], p. 245)

Instead of responding to God, people oppose Him.

Exactly what charge is brought against humankind for the crime of rejecting God? This: "Even though they knew God, they did not honor Him as God" (v. 21). The worst crime ever committed in the universe is the failure to give God glory or credit for who He is. But that is the essence of fallen men and women. When people refuse to recognize the divine attributes of God and that He alone is worthy of exaltation, honor, adoration, and praise, they have committed the ultimate effrontery against God.

The *Westminster Shorter Catechism* states eloquently, "The chief end of mankind is to glorify God and to enjoy Him forever" (cf. Ps. 148; 1 Cor. 10:31). But glorifying Him is precisely what sinful men and women by nature will not do.

FLEEING FROM GOD'S WRATH

The apostle Paul wrote, "All have sinned and fall short of the glory of God" (Rom. 3:23). That's how he characterized the entire human race, apart from regeneration. People refuse to honor God and give Him thanks for all He has provided. Instead, they tend to credit their own power and ingenuity (Deut. 8:10-18). That was particularly true of a certain king in Babylon.

Nebuchadnezzar was one of the greatest monarchs in the history of the world. As king of a mighty empire, he became proud and set himself up as God. He had a ninety-foot image of himself built out of gold and forced the people to bow down and worship it (Dan. 3:5). Such was the strength of Nebuchadnezzar's ego.

However, the king later testified that God broke his pride,

humbled him, and turned his heart toward Him in faith. That all began when the king had a dream. In his own words he tells what happened:

> *I, Nebuchadnezzar, was at ease in my house and flourishing in my palace. I saw a dream and it made me fearful; and these fantasies as I lay on my bed and the visions in my mind kept alarming me.*
> —DAN. 4:4-5

The Aramaic word here translated "ease" means that the king was free from apprehension and fear. At that time his kingdom had no significant internal problems or external opposition. And he was prospering; "flourishing" means that his life was literally "growing green."

The dream, however, caused him to panic, forcing him out of his peaceful condition. In fear he summoned help, calling upon the wise men of the court to interpret his dream. But they were unable to do so.

At last Daniel, a godly Jewish captive who rose to prominence in Nebuchadnezzar's administration, appeared before the king. He replied respectfully, "My lord, if only the dream applied to those who hate you and its interpretation to your adversaries!" (v. 19). What was the meaning of the dream? That Nebuchadnezzar would be humiliated for seven years. He would become insane and act like an animal. But he would not die. After seven years he would reclaim his throne once again, but only after learning that every kingdom belongs to God, the Ruler of everything. Anyone who rules does so only because God has ordained it (Rom. 13:1).

After interpreting the dream, Daniel said, "O king, may my advice be pleasing to you: break away now from your sins by doing righteousness and from your iniquities by showing mercy to the poor, in case there may be a prolonging of your prosperity" (v. 27). Daniel was calling for Nebuchadnezzar to repent of his sin, enter into a righteous relationship with God, and begin to live a merciful life.

But the king refused to do so. A year later, everything happened as Daniel had predicted. Nebuchadnezzar explained what he learned when the seven years were up:

> *I, Nebuchadnezzar, raised my eyes toward heaven and my reason returned to me, and I blessed the Most High and praised and honored Him who lives forever; for His dominion is an everlasting dominion, and His kingdom endures from generation to generation. All the inhabitants of the earth are accounted as nothing, but He does according to His will in the host of heaven and among the inhabitants of earth; and no one can ward off His hand or say to Him, "What have You done?"* ... *Now I, Nebuchadnezzar, praise, exalt and honor the King of heaven, for all His works are true and His ways just, and He is able to humble those who walk in pride.*
>
> —vv. 34-35, 37

What a transformation! Nebuchadnezzar finally understood and accepted God's message. Instead of rejecting God, He glorified Him. Like Nebuchadnezzar, all lost persons need to understand that God is exceedingly angry with them. They must accept the reality that they stand in inevitable judgment before a holy God who *must* react to their sin.

What about you? Will you be like Daniel and warn the lost to flee God's wrath? Like Jonathan Edwards, may this be your message:

> Let every one that is yet out of Christ, and hanging over the pit of hell, whether they be old men and women, or middle aged, or young people, or little children, now hearken to the loud calls of God's word and providence. ... Awake and fly from the wrath to come. (*Sinners in the Hands of an Angry God*, p. 32)

THE GOODNESS OF OUR GOD

When the Pilgrims arrived in Plymouth, Massachusetts in 1620, the first dreadful winter killed nearly half the colony. But those who survived that deadly winter were treated to a summer of plenty. Fish, venison, turkey, Indian corn, barley, peas, and much more were bountiful. Because God had been so good to them, the Pilgrims decided to have a time of prayer and celebration that we know as Thanksgiving. Aside from the traditional fare, their menu included geese, duck, venison, clams, eel, leeks, succotash, watercress, wild plums, and corn bread.

The Plymouth colonists are not the only ones who have acknowledged God's goodness. Throughout biblical history we find individuals who readily spoke of God as being good. When King Hezekiah of Judah prayed for his people, he said, "May the good LORD pardon everyone who prepares his heart to seek God, the LORD God of his fathers" (2 Chron. 30:18-19). During the postexilic era, when the temple foundation was laid, the priests and Levites offered praise and thanksgiving to the Lord, saying, "He is good, for His lovingkindness is upon Israel forever" (Ezra 3:11). Ezra successfully journeyed from Babylon to Jerusalem "because the good hand of his God was upon him" (7:9). "The LORD is good," declared Nahum the prophet (Nahum 1:7). In the New Testament, Jesus Christ characterized Himself as "the good shepherd" (John 10:14).

What exactly does the goodness of God refer to? Charles Hodge wrote:

> Goodness, in the Scriptural sense of the term, includes benevolence, love, mercy, and grace. By benevolence is meant the disposition to promote happiness; all sensitive creatures are its objects. Love includes complacency, desire, and delight, and has rational beings for its objects. Mercy is kindness exercised towards the miserable and includes pity, compassion, forbearance, and gentleness. . . . Grace is love exercised towards the unworthy. . . . All these elements of goodness . . . exist in God without measure and without end. In Him they are infinite, eternal, and immutable. (*Systematic Theology* [Grand Rapids, Mich.: Baker, 1988], pp. 156-157)

It is sad that most people do not acknowledge the goodness of God. They wonder how He can allow bad things to happen, but they don't understand that His goodness prevents us from falling over dead whenever we commit a sin. Because of the Fall, God has every right to wipe out the human race. Only because of His goodness are we able to keep breathing. This is a case of mercy triumphing over judgment (Jas. 2:13).

In the book of Romans Paul asked, "Do you think lightly of the riches of His kindness and tolerance and patience, not knowing that the kindness of God leads you to repentance?" (2:4). To "think lightly of" speaks of grossly underestimating the value or significance of something. It is the failure to assess true worth. What do people underestimate? "The riches of His kindness." That refers to all of God's benefits—His goodness to humankind.

Every person on the face of the earth has personally experienced the goodness of God in many ways. After all, "He causes His sun to rise on the evil and the good, and sends rain on the righteous and the unrighteous" (Matt. 5:45). God provides us with food to eat, heat to keep warm, and water to quench our thirst. He gives us blue sky, green grass, and beautiful mountains. He gives us people to love, and to love us. Yet so often we take all of those blessings for granted and are not thankful.

It is a sinful human tendency to make light of God's "tolerance and patience" (Rom. 2:4). The Greek word translated "tolerance" refers to a truce, a cessation of hostilities, or a withholding of judgment. "Patience" depicts someone who has the power to avenge but doesn't. For long periods God withholds His judgment because He is "compassionate and gracious, slow to anger, and abounding in lovingkindness and truth" (Exod. 34:6; cf. Neh. 9:17; Ps. 103:8; Joel 2:13; Jonah 4:2). This is a common theme in Scripture.

If you as a Christian have ever thought that God is unjust, you have revealed how easy it is to abuse the goodness of God. His goodness is designed to bring about repentance—to cause us to long for Him and to make us thankful that He allows us to live in spite of our sin. Peter wrote, "The Lord is . . . patient toward you, not wishing for any to perish but for all to come to repentance. But the day of the Lord will come" (2 Pet. 3:9-10). Our good God is patient, but not forever—a day of accountability will come.

What kind of response has the goodness of God produced in your life? Are you consistently thankful for what He has provided for you? Or have you forgotten the Provider and become indifferent to Him?

Perhaps pride has led you, like it did the Israelites, to believe that the achievements and blessings you enjoy are from your own hand instead of His (cf. Deut. 8:10-18). We must humbly acknowledge that "every good thing given and every perfect gift is from above, coming down from the Father" (Jas. 1:17). How David did that is a good model to follow:

> Bless the LORD, O my soul,
> And all that is within me, bless His holy name.
> Bless the LORD, O my soul,

> *And forget none of His benefits;*
> *Who pardons all your iniquities,*
> *Who heals all your diseases;*
> *Who redeems your life from the pit,*
> *Who crowns you with loving-kindness*
>   *and compassion;*
> *Who satisfies your years with good things,*
> *So that your youth is renewed like the eagle.*
> —Ps. 103:1-5

THE SUPREME EXPRESSION OF GOD'S GOODNESS

Christ's death on the cross demonstrates the goodness of God like no other event in history. Indeed, it is the supreme expression of His goodness. Let's take a closer look at it in the light of God's love. You may see some things you've never seen before.

The King Over All Endures Mockery

The Gospel of John says that Pilate, the Roman governor of Judea, "took Jesus and scourged Him" (John 19:1). Instead of releasing Christ, whom he repeatedly pronounced innocent, Pilate tried to satiate the mob's thirst for blood by having Him scourged. A Roman scourge had a short wooden handle that held a series of leather thongs threaded with bits of lead, brass, and bones sharpened to a razor's edge. Scourging often brought about death, and it was usually done before crucifixion to speed up the victim's death on the cross. It was torture beyond description.

The Jews gave forty lashes, save one. We don't know how many the Romans administered. We do know that Christ had been so badly beaten, He couldn't carry His own cross all the way to the place of execution.

Following the scourging but before the crucifixion, "the soldiers of the governor took Jesus into the Praetorium and gathered the whole Roman cohort around Him. They stripped Him and put a scarlet robe on Him. And after twisting together a crown of thorns, they put it on His head, and a reed in His right hand; and they knelt down before Him and mocked Him, saying, 'Hail, King of the Jews!'" (Matt. 27:27-29). Historians tell us that Roman soldiers commonly did this as a cruel game, to make sport of those they considered to be mentally deranged.

Then the soldiers "spat on Him, and took the reed and began to beat Him on the head. After they had mocked Him, they took the scarlet robe off Him and put His own garments back on Him" (vv. 30-31). In taking off the robe, they were opening fresh wounds. In putting back on His garments, they brought about excruciating pain, for the common man's clothing in that day was made of coarse fibers.

The Lord of Life Endures Crucifixion

The Roman soldiers then led Christ away to be crucified. The procession would have gone like this: Four Roman soldiers surrounded the prisoner, one at each corner, moving him through the city, with other soldiers before and behind. The soldiers would parade the prisoner down the main streets. On the day of Christ's crucifixion, the streets would have been swelled with pilgrims coming to worship and celebrate the Passover. Either hanging from the prisoner's neck or held by someone walking in front was a placard explaining why the prisoner was being executed. That way the people would know the price of that particular crime.

As the procession came out of the city, it was apparent that the strength of Christ was giving out. So the soldiers conscripted a man in the crowd, Simon of Cyrene, to carry the cross of Christ to the place of execution. Simon was a direct beneficiary of God's greatest display of goodness, for he eventually became a believer. In Mark 15:21, the Gospel writer made that obvious by listing the names of Simon's children, evidently mentioned because the church at large knew them.

When the procession arrived at Golgotha, the soldiers gave Christ "wine to drink mixed with gall; and after tasting it, He was unwilling to drink" (Matt. 27:34). The Greek word for "gall" is a general term that refers to something bitter. The Gospel of Mark specifies that the myrrh was mixed with wine. Myrrh is a bitter gum resin that was put into wine for the purpose of calming a person. In the first century it was thought to have narcotic properties.

The soldiers didn't seek to drug the victim as an act of mercy; they didn't care whether the victim suffered or not. The drug simply made their task easier because it would be difficult to hammer nails through someone's limbs if that person weren't drugged to some degree. But Christ refused to drink the drugged mixture. Not wanting any of His senses to be dulled, He was committed to enduring the full pain of the cross.

The soldiers then crucified Christ. According to William Barclay, crucifixion "originated in Persia. . . . The earth was considered to be sacred to Ormuzd the god, and the criminal was lifted up from it that he might not defile the earth, which was the god's property. From Persia crucifixion passed to Carthage in North Africa; and it was from Carthage that Rome learned it" (*The Gospel of Matthew*, Vol. 2 [Philadelphia: Westminster, 1958], p. 402).

The Gospel writers didn't give the details of what happened, but it's helpful to have some understanding of what Christ endured on the cross. The soldiers first laid the cross on the ground and then placed Him on it. They extended His feet, pulling His toes down. They drove a large nail through the arch of one foot and then through the other.

After they extended His hands, allowing His knees to flex a little, they drove two great nails through His wrists—not His palms—just below the heel of each hand. Once the soldiers had nailed Christ to the cross, they lifted the cross and dropped it into a hole. When it hit bottom, the shock would have caused Him great pain. He was now crucified.

In his book *The Life of Christ*, scholar Frederic Farrar wrote:

> A death by crucifixion seems to include all that pain and death can have of the horrible and ghastly—dizziness, cramp, thirst, starvation, sleeplessness, traumatic fever, tetanus, publicity of shame, long continuance of torment, horror of anticipation, mortification of untended wounds—all intensified just up to the point at which they can be endured at all, but all stopping just short of the point which would give to the sufferer the relief of unconsciousness.
>
> The unnatural position made every movement painful; the lacerated veins and crushed tendons throbbed with incessant anguish; the wounds, inflamed by exposure, gradually gangrened; the arteries—especially of the head and stomach—became swollen and oppressed with surcharged blood; and while each variety of misery went on gradually increasing, there was added to them the intolerable pang of a burning and raging thirst; and all these physical complications caused an internal excitement and anxiety, which made the prospect of death itself—of death, the awful unknown enemy, at whose approach man usually shudders most—bear the aspect of a delicious and exquisite release. ([Portland: Fountain, 1976], p. 641)

The authorities did not seek a quick, painless death to preserve a small measure of dignity for the criminal. On the contrary, they sought an agonizing torture to humiliate him completely. Such was the suffering that our Lord Jesus Christ, out of His goodness, experienced.

Even Christ's suffering on the cross was not enough to satiate the evil desire of His enemies—they had to torment Him as well. Matthew described it this way:

> *And those passing by were hurling abuse at Him, wagging their heads and saying, "You who are going to destroy the temple*

*and rebuild it in three days, save Yourself! If You are the Son
of God, come down from the cross."*

*In the same way the chief priests also, along with the scribes
and elders, were mocking Him and saying, "He saved others;
He cannot save Himself. He is the King of Israel; let Him now
come down from the cross, and we will believe in Him. He
trusts in God; let Him rescue Him now, if He delights in Him."
. . . The robbers who had been crucified with Him were also
insulting Him with the same words.*

—27:39-44

About midafternoon Christ cried out with a loud voice, saying, "My God, My God, why have You forsaken Me?" (v. 46).
Here is something completely beyond human understanding:
God became separated from God. God the Father turned His
back on God the Son.

Exactly what kind of separation was that? The Son wasn't
separated from His own divine nature—He didn't cease to be
God. Neither was He separated from the Trinity in essence or
substance. Rather, He was separated in terms of intimate fellowship and communion with the Father.

Finally Christ declared, "It is finished!" and "bowed His
head and gave up His spirit" (John 19:30). The suffering He so
willingly endured for the sake of mankind was over.

Why Did He Do It?

Why did God allow His own Son to die on a cross? Paul
explained, "He who did not spare His own Son, but delivered
Him up *for us all*, how will He not also with Him freely give
us all things?" (Rom. 8:32, emphasis added). In His condem-
nation and death, Christ took our place. Isaiah said of Christ,
"He was pierced through for *our* transgressions, He was
crushed for *our* iniquities; the chastening for *our* well-being fell
upon Him, and by His scourging *we* are healed. *All of us* like

sheep have gone astray, *each of us* has turned to his own way; but the LORD has caused the iniquity of *us all* to fall on Him" (53:5-6, emphasis added).

The Father "made Him who knew no sin to be sin on our behalf, so that we might become the righteousness of God in Him" (2 Cor. 5:21). Christ "redeemed us from the curse of the Law, having become a curse for us" (Gal. 3:13).

The death of Christ is a demonstration of what God is like. Paul said, "God demonstrates His own love toward us, in that while we were yet sinners, Christ died for us" (Rom. 5:8). One of the most beautiful and moving hymns about the cross is "O Sacred Head, Now Wounded," which is attributed to Bernard of Clairvaux in the twelfth century. Read the words prayerfully and reverently, for they tell of a God who deeply loves us:

> *O sacred Head, now wounded,*
> *With grief and shame weighed down.*
> *Now scornfully surrounded*
> *With thorns, Thine only crown;*
> *O sacred Head, what glory,*
> *What bliss till now was Thine!*
> *Yet, though despised and gory,*
> *I joy to call Thee mine.*
>
> *What Thou, my Lord, hast suffered*
> *Was all for sinners' gain.*
> *Mine, mine was the transgression,*
> *But Thine the deadly pain.*
> *Lo, here I fall, my Saviour!*
> *'Tis I deserve Thy place;*
> *Look on me with Thy favor,*
> *Vouchsafe to me Thy grace.*
>
> *What language shall I borrow*
> *To thank Thee, dearest Friend,*
> *For this Thy dying sorrow,*

> *Thy pity without end?*
> *O make me Thine forever;*
> *And should I fainting be,*
> *Lord, let me never, never*
> *Outlive my love to Thee.*

THE BELIEVER'S CONFIDENCE

"Who will separate us from the love of Christ?" asked Paul. "Will tribulation, or distress, or persecution, or famine, or nakedness, or peril, or sword?" (Rom. 8:35). That's a reference to Christ's love for us, not our love for Christ. It was Paul's way of emphasizing the goodness of God in the believer's life. Paul was saying, "What can make Christ stop loving you?" The obvious answer is: *Nothing.*

Paul went on to specify various afflictions that might cause a believer to question God's goodness. "Tribulation" speaks of pressure from external difficulties. That includes suffering from false accusations, rejection, or bodily harm. Paul knew all about that from experience, for he said:

> *Five times I received from the Jews thirty-nine lashes. Three times I was beaten with rods, once I was stoned, three times I was shipwrecked, a night and a day I have spent in the deep. I have been on frequent journeys, in dangers from rivers, dangers from robbers, dangers from my countrymen, dangers from the Gentiles, dangers in the city, dangers in the wilderness, dangers on the sea, dangers among false brethren; I have been in labor and hardship, through many sleepless nights, in hunger and thirst, often without food, in cold and exposure.*
>
> —2 COR. 11:24-27

Those trials never broke the bond of Christ's love for Paul, and no adversity will ever separate you from Christ's love either.

Paul also spoke of "distress" (Rom. 8:35). As mentioned earlier, the Greek term refers to internal pressure and literally means "narrowness of room." It pictures someone who is caught in a narrow space or is hemmed in with no way out. It can specifically refer to temptation. Does your experiencing extreme distress or temptation mean that God no longer loves you? No! God promises that when you undergo such pressure, He will enable you to endure it and will at the right time provide a way out (1 Cor. 10:13).

What about the other afflictions? What if you suffer at the hands of those who reject Christ? What if you go without food, even to the point of starvation? What about a lack of clothing or shelter? Are those adversities evidence that God is not good, that He does not love you anymore? Absolutely not! Remember, it is impossible for anyone or anything to separate you from God's love.

It's no wonder Paul prayed that we as believers would comprehend the breadth, length, height, and depth of God's love (Eph. 3:18-19). How broad is His love? Broad enough to reconcile Jew and Gentile and make them one in Christ (2:13-14). How long is His love? Long enough to stretch from eternity past (1:4). How deep is His love? Deep enough to reach us when we were dead in our trespasses and sin (2:1-5). How high is His love? High enough to raise us up and seat us in heaven with Him (2:6).

Its breadth—it can reach anyone. Its length—it runs from eternity to eternity. Its depth—it reaches to the pit of sin. Its height—it takes us to the presence of God and seats us on His throne. That is the love and goodness we are to know and build our lives on.

9

OUR SOVEREIGN GOD

Lady Jane Kenmure was intimately acquainted with sorrow and adversity. In 1600 she was born into a distinguished Scottish family and later married Sir John Gordon, who became Lord Kenmure. Many undoubtedly envied her social prestige, but great difficulty marked the life of this humble and devout believer. When she had been married for eight years, she had already lost three young daughters. In the same year that her third child died, her husband lay in the throes of death, and he too passed away. A month or two after that, she joyfully gave birth to a son, but four years later the boy became sick and also died. About a year later she remarried, but her happiness was short-lived, for her second husband died soon thereafter.

During Lady Kenmure's extended time of sorrow, Samuel Rutherford, her minister, wrote pastoral letters to comfort her. Note how he guided her to think on the goodness of God:

> Be content to wade through the waters betwixt you and glory with Him, holding His hand fast, for He knoweth all the fords. . . . When ye are got up thither, and have cast your eyes to view the golden city . . . ye shall then say, "Four-and twenty hours' abode in this place is worth threescore and ten years' sorrow upon earth." . . .
>
> God aimeth in all His dealings with His children to bring them to a high contempt of and deadly feud with the world;

to set a high price upon Christ, and to think Him One who cannot be bought for gold, and well worthy the fighting for. And for no other cause . . . doth the Lord withdraw from you the childish toys and earthly delights that He giveth unto others but that He may have you wholly to Himself. . . .

Subscribe to the Almighty's will. . . . Let the cross of your Lord Jesus have your submissive and resolute AMEN. . . .

I confess it seemed strange to me, that your Lord should have done that which seemed to [knock] out the bottom of your worldly comforts; but we see not the ground of the Almighty's sovereignty. "He goeth by on our right hand, and on our left hand, and we see Him not." We see but pieces of the broken links of the chains of His providence. (*The Letters of Samuel Rutherford*, edited by S. Maxwell Coder and Wilbur M. Smith [Chicago: Moody, 1951], pp. 63, 66, 390-391)

In essence, Pastor Rutherford was directing Lady Kenmure to focus on the sovereignty of God. That God is sovereign means that He does as He pleases and only as He pleases. No person or circumstance can defeat His counsel or thwart His purposes.

Scripture is full of evidence that God acts according to His sovereign pleasure. Job said to the Lord, "I know that You can do all things, and that no purpose of Yours can be thwarted" (Job 42:2). The psalmist said, "Whatever the LORD pleases, He does, in heaven and in earth, in the seas and in all deeps" (Ps. 135:6). "My purpose will be established," said God, "and I will accomplish all My good pleasure" (Isa. 46:10).

God is sovereign. Let's see how that attribute affects the life of a believer. First, God sovereignly exercises His option as Creator of all to select certain individuals to receive His divine mercy.

There are three theological senses in which He chooses or elects. The first is *theocratic election*. That refers to God's selection of a nation to be His covenant people. Moses said to the Israelites, "You are a holy people to the LORD your God; the

LORD your God has chosen you to be a people for His own pos-
session out of all the peoples who are on the face of the earth. . . .
Know, then, it is not because of your righteousness that the
LORD your God is giving you this good land to possess" (Deut.
7:6; 9:6). God freely chose them out of His love and grace, and
not because of any merit on their part.

The second sense is *vocational election*. God sometimes
chooses particular individuals to do specific tasks. God chose
Moses to lead Israel from Egypt and chose the Levites to serve
the nation as the priestly tribe. In the New Testament Christ
chose twelve of His followers to be apostles.

The third sense is *salvational election*. God selects certain
individuals for salvation. Peter wrote to persecuted believers
who were "chosen according to the foreknowledge of God" (1
Pet. 1:1-2). In addition, Paul explained that God "chose us in
Him [Christ] before the foundation of the world" (Eph. 1:4).

God formed the body of Christ by His independent,
sovereign choice. His choice was totally apart from any human
consideration and purely on the basis of His own will. We were
chosen "according to the kind intention of His will" (v. 5) and
"according to His purpose who works all things after the counsel of His will" (v. 11). God sovereignly and freely chose us to
be included in the church.

When did God choose us for salvation? "Before the foundation of the world" (v. 4). That means we were chosen before the
creation of the universe—chosen in eternity past. A day is coming when Christ will proclaim, "Come, you who are blessed of
My Father, inherit the kingdom prepared for you from the foundation of the world" (Matt. 25:34).

Why did God choose us? Because He loves us. Paul said,
"God, being rich in mercy, because of His great love with which
He loved us, even when we were dead in our transgressions,
made us alive together with Christ" (Eph. 2:4-5).

God's sovereign, saving work is foundational to His

promise to work all things together for our good (Rom. 8:28). That is the most glorious promise imaginable. Nothing could be more reassuring. Nothing could bring more hope, joy, trust, confidence, happiness, and freedom for the believer than to know that God will sovereignly work everything in his or her life for good.

The Greek term translated "good" refers to something that is morally or inherently good, not to something that just has a nice outward appearance. In saying all things work together for good, Paul had two things in mind: our current circumstances and our future glorification. No matter what happens in our lives, God will sovereignly work things out to produce something immediately and ultimately beneficial for us. That is true regarding everything we experience in life, both good and bad.

GOOD THINGS WORK FOR OUR GOOD

What kind of good things work for our spiritual benefit? To start with, God's attributes. God's power, for example, supports us in the midst of trouble. God supported Daniel when he was in a lions' den, Jonah when he was in a fish's belly, and three Hebrew men when they were thrown into a furnace. When God delivered David from the murderous hand of King Saul, David declared, "'I love You, O LORD, my strength.' The LORD is my rock and my fortress and my deliverer, my God, my rock, in whom I take refuge; my shield and the horn of my salvation, my stronghold" (Ps. 18:1-2). In Christ we are "strengthened with all power, according to His glorious might" (Col. 1:11).

God's power also supports us when we lack strength. Paul observed God's strength on display in his own weaknesses (2 Cor. 12:9). God truly "gives strength to the weary, and to him who lacks might He increases power. Though youths grow weary and tired, and vigorous young men stumble badly, yet those who wait for the LORD will gain new strength; they will mount up with wings like eagles, they will run and not get tired, they will walk and not become weary" (Isa. 40:29-31). When we lack strength, God infuses us with His.

God's promises, in addition to His attributes, work out for our good. His promise to forgive our sins is one example. David wrote, "As far as the east is from the west, so far has He removed our transgressions from us" (Ps. 103:12). "You have cast all my sins behind Your back," said Isaiah (38:17). Micah, speaking of God's forgiveness toward His people, wrote, "He will again have compassion on us; He will tread our iniquities under foot. Yes, You will cast all their sins into the depths of the sea" (Mic. 7:19). God Himself said, "I, even I, am the one who wipes out your transgressions for My own sake, and I will not remember your sins" (Isa. 43:25).

What else works for our good? God's Word: "All Scripture is inspired by God and profitable for teaching, for reproof, for correction, for training in righteousness; that the man of God may be adequate, equipped for every good work" (2 Tim. 3:16-17). The Greek word translated "teaching" refers to the body of doctrinal truth that is to govern our thoughts and actions. "Reproof" speaks of exposing sinful conduct and erroneous teaching. "Correction" means "to straighten up" or "to lift up." Scripture can restore us to a proper spiritual posture. "Training in righteousness" refers to Scripture's ability to bring us to maturity. God uses His Word for our good because it provides all that we need to live a godly life.

BAD THINGS WORK OUT FOR OUR GOOD

While it is important to know that good things work for our good, Paul's primary focus in Romans 8 is on bad things working out for our good. Note carefully, however: We are not to redefine bad and pretend it is good. God hates that. In Isaiah 5:20 He says, "Woe to those who call evil good, and good evil; who substitute darkness for light and light for darkness; who substitute bitter for sweet and sweet for bitter!"

Bad things are always inherently evil. Sin is sin, evil is evil, and neither will ever change. Yet we can be confident that God sovereignly overrules whatever is bad to work it out for our good in the long run. That includes suffering, temptation, and even sin.

Suffering

Suffering is a result of the curse. If sin had not been introduced into the world, there would be no suffering, pain, sorrow, or death. Although suffering itself is not evil, it is the result of an evil world.

One of the first biblical examples we have of God working out such evil for good is the suffering of Joseph. His brothers threw him into a pit and then later sold him to some men on their way to Egypt (Gen. 37:20-28). Later he was unjustly imprisoned. But God enabled Joseph to interpret a dream for Pharaoh and warn him of a coming famine. As a result, Pharaoh made Joseph prime minister of Egypt. Because God placed Joseph in that position, he was able to provide food for his family as well as for all the people of Egypt. Even though his brothers had sold him into slavery, Joseph could later say to them, "You meant evil against me, but God meant it for good in order to bring about this present result, to preserve many people alive" (50:20). He realized that the injustices he had suffered were a part of God's sovereign plan for his life.

What about us? Does God actually use our suffering for good? Absolutely. One benefit of suffering is that it teaches us to hate sin. When Christ went to the tomb of Lazarus, He "was deeply moved in spirit and was troubled" (John 11:33). He agonized over the tears, pain, and sorrow that sin and death bring. When we experience suffering, we learn to hate the sin that brings it about.

Suffering also works for our good because it exposes the sin in our lives. When everything is fine, it's easy to feel pious. But as soon as things collapse and trouble comes our way, there's a greater temptation to become angry with God. We can easily lose our patience and begin to doubt His goodness. That's when a person finds out whether he or she really trusts God, for suffering will expose any evil in the heart.

Suffering not only exposes sin, but also drives it out. It is a fire that burns away our dross and reveals the pure gold and silver. Job said of God, "He knows the way I take; when He has tried me, I shall come forth as gold" (Job 23:10).

How else does suffering work for our good? It reveals that we indeed are His children. After all, "'Those whom the Lord loves He disciplines, and He scourges every son whom He receives.' It is for discipline that you endure; God deals with you as with sons; for what son is there whom his father does not discipline? But if you are without discipline, of which all have become partakers, then you are illegitimate children and not sons" (Heb. 12:6-8). His discipline is evidence that we are His children.

Suffering also drives us to God. In prosperity the heart is easily divided. That's why God warned the Israelites not to forget Him when He brought them into the Promised Land (Deut. 6:10-13). Suffering forces us to stop focusing on the world. When everything in our lives is comfortable, we're apt to be preoccupied with our house, car, job, business, or wardrobe. But suppose a loved one becomes terminally ill. That would change our values and drive us to God, which is a good response to a tragic situation. Paul's "thorn in the flesh" drove him to the Lord (2 Cor. 12:7-10).

Whatever our afflictions might be, we can be assured that God is sovereignly using them for our good. With that as her theme, Margaret Clarkson wrote a book for those who live their lives in perpetual pain. She titled it *Grace Grows Best in Winter*, a quote from the letters of Samuel Rutherford, the minister who sought to comfort the suffering lady described at the beginning of this chapter. Clarkson's subtitle is *Help for Those Who Must Suffer*, and one of her many helpful observations is this:

> The sovereignty of God is the one impregnable rock to which the suffering human heart must cling. The circumstances surrounding our lives are no accident: they may be the work of evil, but that evil is held firmly within the mighty hand of our sovereign God. . . . All evil is subject to Him, and evil cannot touch His children unless He permits it. God is the Lord of human history and of the personal history of every member of His redeemed family. . . . He does not explain His actions to us any more than He did to Job, but He has given us what the sufferers of old never had—the written revelation of His sovereignty and love and His manifestation of Himself in the Savior. If those saints could triumph so gloriously without such revelation, shall we who have it go down to defeat? ([Grand Rapids, Mich.: Zondervan, 1972], pp. 40-41)

Temptation

Temptation too works for our good. The main reason is that it makes us depend on God. When an animal sees a hunter, it runs for safety. Similarly, when the devil shoots his fiery darts, we are to flee to God's throne of grace, that He might protect us. Struggling against temptation causes us to see how weak we really are and to realize that we have no reason to be proud of ourselves. That forces us to follow Paul's example and lean on the strength of Christ (2 Cor. 12:9-10; Phil. 4:11-13).

Our Lord Jesus knew what temptation was all about, for Scripture says of Him, "We do not have a high priest who cannot sympathize with our weaknesses, but One who has been tempted in all things as we are, yet without sin. Let us therefore draw near with confidence to the throne of grace, so that we may receive mercy and may find grace to help in time of need" (Heb. 4:15-16). Because Christ Himself experienced great temptation, He understands what we go through and is therefore able to help us in our struggles. Similarly, our dealing with temptation enables us to help others in their struggles (cf. Gal. 6:1).

Temptation also works for our good because it makes us desire heaven. Perhaps at times we can relate to Paul's frustration: "The good that I want, I do not do, but I practice the very evil that I do not want. . . . Wretched man that I am! Who will set me free from the body of this death?" (Rom. 7:19, 24). At times like that we long for heaven, saying with Paul, "To me, to live is Christ and to die is gain" (Phil. 1:21). Paul had a balanced perspective, however, for he went on to say, "I am hard-pressed from both directions, having the desire to depart and be with Christ, for that is very much better; yet to remain on in the flesh is more necessary for your sake" (vv. 23-24). Being involved in a ministry that needs us will motivate us to carry on in spite of whatever trials and temptations we experience.

Sin

God promises that *all* things will ultimately work out for our good, and that includes the worst thing of all: sin. His promise doesn't lessen the ugliness of sin or the beauty of holiness. Sin is intrinsically wicked and deserving of eternal hell. But in His infinite wisdom God overrules it for our good. How?

When we see sin and its effects in other people, we sense a holy indignation against it. That leads us to be stronger in our opposition to evil. We also become more thankful that the Lord has delivered us from sins in our own lives.

When we become aware of sin in our own experience, the Holy Spirit prods us to examine our heart in the light of God's Word. We should ask God to search our souls to find any latent sin, just as we would want a physician to find any latent cancer. An appropriate remedy cannot be prescribed before the malady is known. That's why Job cried out to God, "Make known to me my rebellion and my sin" (Job 13:23). It is better that we find out our sins than that they find us out. And we must make it a lifetime habit, when we do become aware of personal sin, to extricate it immediately.

The threat of sin also compels us to be spiritually alert. Our heart is like a castle that is in danger of assault every hour from the world, the flesh, and the devil. Because that is so, we are to be like a soldier who is ever alert for an attack from the enemy.

Although God sovereignly causes our sin to work for good, we should never view that wonderful promise as a license to sin. In his book *All Things for Good*, Thomas Watson warned:

> If any of God's people should be tampering with sin, because God can turn it to good, though the Lord does not damn them, He may send them to hell in this life. He may put them into such bitter agonies and soul-convulsions, as may fill them full of horror, and make them draw nigh to despair. Let this be a flaming sword to keep them from coming near the forbidden tree. ([Carlisle, Penn.: The Banner of Truth Trust, 1986], p. 51)

Paul put it like this: "What shall we say then? Are we to continue in sin so that grace may increase? May it never be! How shall we who died to sin still live in it? . . . our old self was crucified with Him [Christ], in order that our body of sin might be done away with, so that we would no longer be slaves to sin" (Rom. 6:1-2, 6).

Why does God promise to work everything out for our good? Because He wants to conform us into the image of His Son (Rom. 8:29). Making us like Christ is the destiny to which He sovereignly appointed us before the world began. Since nothing can thwart His sovereign purposes, we can be "confident of this very thing, that He who began a good work in [us] will perfect it until the day of Christ Jesus" (Phil. 1:6).

10

OUR FATHER GOD

As mentioned in a previous chapter, Helen Keller is one of the most remarkable women in history. On the advice of Dr. Alexander Graham Bell, her parents sent for a teacher from the Perkins Institution for the Blind in Boston. Anne Sullivan, a nineteen-year-old orphan, was chosen for the task of instructing six-year-old Helen. It was the beginning of a close and lifelong friendship between them.

By means of a manual alphabet, Anne "spelled" into Helen's hand such words as *doll* or *puppy*. Two years later Helen was reading and writing Braille fluently. At ten Helen learned different sounds by placing her fingers on her teacher's larynx and "hearing" the vibrations. Later Helen went to Radcliffe College, where Anne "spelled" the lectures into Helen's hand. After graduating with honors, Helen decided to devote her life to helping the blind and deaf. As part of that endeavor, she wrote many books and articles and traveled around the world making speeches. Since Helen's speeches were not intelligible to some, Anne often translated them for her.

Their nearly fifty years of companionship ended when Anne died in 1936. Helen wrote these endearing words about her lifelong friend:

My teacher is so near to me that I scarcely think of myself apart from her. . . . I feel that her being is inseparable from my own, and that the footsteps of my life are in hers. All the best of me belongs to her—there is not a talent, or an aspiration or a joy in me that has not been awakened by her loving touch. (*The Story of My Life* [New York: Doubleday, 1954], p. 47)

It's obvious that Anne knew Helen better than anyone. In the spiritual realm, Christ knows God better than anyone. Better than theologians who have written about Him through the centuries. Even better than the prophets and apostles, who received divine revelation. Christ knows God so well because He was in God's presence from before eternity. The apostle John said it this way: "In the beginning was the Word, and the Word was with God" (John 1:1). Christ was face to face with God. If anyone knows about God, Christ does.

It stands to reason, therefore, that if we really want to know what God is like, we ought to listen to what Christ said about Him. To begin with, He spoke of God's *holiness*, addressing Him as "holy Father" (John 17:11) and "righteous Father" (v. 25). He spoke of God's *justice*, telling a parable about rendering due penalty to tenant farmers who killed the landowner's son in an attempt to gain his inheritance (Matt. 21:33-46). He spoke of God's *power*, pointing out that "all things are possible with God" (Mark 10:27). He spoke of God's *sovereignty*, saying, "Your kingdom come. Your will be done, on earth as it is in heaven" (Matt. 6:10). He spoke of God's *omniscience*, saying He is a "Father who sees what is done in secret" (6:4). He spoke of God's *goodness* and *love*, characterizing Him as a gracious Father who provides all that His dear children need (7:9-11).

Those are all wonderful truths, but there is one theme that surpasses them all. More than any other concept of God, Christ knew God as His *Father*.

THE FATHER'S RELATIONSHIP TO THE SON

What did Christ teach about the fatherhood of God? Listen to what He said:

> *My Father is working until now, and I Myself am working. . . . The Son can do nothing of Himself, unless it is something He sees the Father doing; for whatever the Father does, these things the Son also does in like manner. For the Father loves the Son, and shows Him all things that He Himself is doing; and the Father will show Him greater works than these, so that you will marvel.*
>
> *For just as the Father raises the dead and gives them life, even so the Son also gives life to whom He wishes. For not even the Father judges anyone, but He has given all judgment to the Son, so that all will honor the Son even as they honor the Father. He who does not honor the Son does not honor the Father who sent Him. Truly, truly, I say to you, he who hears My word, and believes Him who sent Me, has eternal life, and does not come into judgment, but has passed out of death into life.*
>
> —JOHN 5:17, 19-24

Why did Christ make this statement about God and Himself? He had just healed a man who had been crippled for thirty-eight years. But because He healed the man on the Sabbath, a day of rest, the religious leaders criticized Him for working. His response to such incredible narrow-mindedness showed His right to heal on the Sabbath. Intermingled with it is His theology on the fatherhood of God. Let's take it apart to see exactly what Jesus was saying.

The Father Is One with His Son

In saying, "My Father is working until now, and I Myself am working" (v. 17), Jesus was saying, "I am one with God. He works on the Sabbath, and I work on the Sabbath. We are equal." Leon Morris explains:

> Here His defense rests on His intimate relationship to the Father. . . . The expression "My Father" is noteworthy. It was not the way Jews usually referred to God. Usually they spoke of "our Father," and while they might use "My Father" in prayer they would qualify it with "in heaven" or some other expression to remove the suggestion of familiarity. Jesus did no such thing, here or elsewhere. He habitually thought of God as in the closest relationship to Himself. (*The Gospel According to John* [Grand Rapids, Mich.: Eerdmans, 1971], pp. 308-309)

Christ's critics clearly understood what He was suggesting. That's why they "were seeking all the more to kill Him, because He . . . was calling God His own Father, making Himself equal with God" (v. 18).

Christ, being omniscient, sensed their murderous thoughts, but nevertheless went on emphasizing His oneness with the Father: "The Son can do nothing of Himself, unless it is something He sees the Father doing; for whatever the Father does, these things the Son also does in like manner" (v. 19). Christ was saying, "The Father and I are one. We work together."

This oneness between the Father and Son is also evident in Christ's high-priestly prayer on behalf of all believers: "My prayer is not for them alone [the disciples]. I pray also for those who will believe in me through their message, that all of them may be one, Father, just as you are in me and I am in you. May they also be in us so that the world may believe that you have sent me. I have given them the glory that you gave me, that they may be one as we are one" (17:20-22, NIV). There was a holy intimacy and communion between the Father and Son.

The Father Loves His Son

What else did Christ teach about God? That "the Father loves
the Son" (John 5:20). Christ was very well aware of the Father's
love, for He went on to pray in His high-priestly prayer, "I in
them [all believers] and you in me. May they be brought to complete unity to let the world know that you sent me and have
loved them even as you have loved me. . . . I have made you
known to them, and will continue to make you known in order
that the love you have for me may be in them and that I myself
may be in them" (17:23, 26, NIV). The Father's love for the Son
is the root of our love for one another as believers.

The Father Blesses His Son

The Father not only loves the Son, but also "shows Him all
things that He Himself is doing" (John 5:20). The union of the
Father and Son results in communication that is perfect and
complete in every way. Christ, for example, knew all the details
of God's redemptive plan, but He "endured the cross" anyway
"for the joy set before Him" (Heb. 12:2).

What was that joy? Again Jesus' high-priestly prayer sheds
light on the nature of the divine relationship. It was the joy of
glorification, which Jesus explained this way: "I have brought
you glory on earth by completing the work you gave me to do.
And now, Father, glorify me in your presence with the glory I
had with you before the world began" (John 17:4-5, NIV). Jesus
glorified the Father by totally exhibiting the Father's attributes
and by fully doing the Father's will. Likewise, we glorify God
when we allow His attributes to shine through our lives and
obey His will in everything we do.

The Father Gives Authority to His Son

What kind of authority does Christ have? "For just as the
Father raises the dead and gives them life, even so the Son also

gives life to whom He wishes. For not even the Father judges anyone, but He has given all judgment to the Son. . . . An hour is coming and now is, when the dead will hear the voice of the Son of God, and those who hear will live. For just as the Father has life in Himself, even so He gave to the Son also to have life in Himself" (John 5:21-22, 25-26). The Father gave authority and power to the Son to rule, reign, and judge. The Son, along with the Father, will raise the dead in the great resurrection on the last day.

The Father Honors His Son

The authority the Son enjoys is equal to that of the Father. The goal, said Christ, is "that all will honor the Son even as they honor the Father. He who does not honor the Son does not honor the Father who sent Him . . . he who hears My Word, and believes Him who sent Me, has eternal life, and does not come into judgment, but has passed out of death into life" (John 5:23-24). All who believe in God as He has revealed Himself to be will also believe in Jesus. It is impossible for someone to believe what the Father says and turn away from the Son. Such is the honor bestowed upon our Lord Jesus Christ.

BELONGING TO GOD'S FAMILY

God is a Father not only to the Son, but also to every believer. J. I. Packer wrote:

> You sum up the whole of New Testament teaching in a single phrase, if you speak of it as a revelation of the Fatherhood of the holy Creator. In the same way, you sum up the whole of New Testament religion if you describe it as the knowledge of God as one's holy Father. If you want to judge how well a person understands Christianity, find out how much he makes of the thought of being God's child, and having God as his Father.

If this is not the thought that prompts and controls his worship and prayers and his whole outlook on life, it means that he does not understand Christianity very well at all. For everything that Christ taught, everything that makes the New Testament new, and better than the Old, everything that is distinctively Christian as opposed to merely Jewish, is summed up in the knowledge of the Fatherhood of God. "Father" is the Christian name for God. (*Knowing God* [Downers Grove, Ill.: InterVarsity, 1973], p. 182)

In Romans 8:14-17, Paul spoke of our adoption into God's family as His children: "All who are being led by the Spirit of God, these are sons of God. . . . [We] have received a spirit of adoption as sons by which we cry out, 'Abba! Father!' The Spirit Himself bears witness with our spirit that we are children of God, and . . . heirs also, heirs of God and fellow heirs with Christ."

Abba is an Aramaic term that means "Daddy" or "Papa." It is a personal term reflecting trust, dependence, intimacy, and love. Once we were sinners living in fear; now we are sons in the care of our heavenly Father. Once we were strangers; now we are intimate friends. Our adoption means that we can come into God's majestic presence and say, "Daddy."

It is the role of the Holy Spirit, the third member of the Trinity, to give us a deep sense of intimacy with the Father. He prompts us to come into God's presence for intimate fellowship—not in fear, but with a sense of freedom and confidence. That makes it easy to share with God the deepest concerns of our hearts. We can say to Him, "I need to talk to You about this problem."

The author of Hebrews spoke of our intimacy with God this way:

Both He who sanctifies [Christ] and those who are sanctified [believers] are all from one Father, for which reason He is not ashamed to call them brethren, saying, "I will proclaim Your name to My brethren, in the midst of the congregation I will sing Your praise."

—2:11-12

Jesus calls us brothers and sisters and sees Himself standing arm in arm with us, singing praises to God!

A PARABLE ABOUT GOD

In the Gospel of Luke is a story Jesus told that is commonly called "The Parable of the Prodigal Son" (15:11-32). That title is a bit misleading because the focus of the parable is on a loving father, not a sinful son. It illustrates the fatherhood of God in a practical way and helps us see what God is really like.

The Wayward Son

The parable is about a man with two sons. Even though the father was still alive, the younger son demanded his share of the inheritance from his father's estate. (It would have been one-third since he was the younger son and the elder son, as the firstborn, received a double portion of the inheritance [cf. Deut. 21:17; from *MacArthur Study Bible*, p. 1545].) Such a request was obviously a show of great disrespect. In fact, according to the customs of the Middle East, it was equivalent to a death wish.

Shortly after receiving his inheritance, the younger son decided to take a journey to a distant country, where he squandered his inheritance on "loose living" (v. 13). The phrase speaks of wastefulness, excess, and wild extravagance. Although we don't know exactly what he did with the inheritance, we do know that he ruined himself by living without restraints and consuming all his fortune.

The younger son then faced a double disaster. After he had spent everything, a severe famine arose in the land and he began to be in extreme need. Since food was scarce and high-priced, no one was giving it away. Subsequently, he worked for a citizen of that country, and his new employer sent him to the fields to feed pigs—unclean animals according to Jewish ceremonial law.

Apparently, neither the employer nor anyone else gave him anything to eat before he went to work. Perhaps the employer valued the pigs more than human life, thinking the animals could at least be eaten or sold for profit. The starving son became so hungry that he wanted to eat pig feed!

The Gracious Father

When disillusionment set in, the younger son finally came to his senses and said, "How many of my father's hired men have more than enough bread, but I am dying here with hunger!" (v. 17). "Hired men" speaks not of household slaves or contracted servants, but of day laborers. He was saying, "Even the people passing down the road whom my father hires for one day's work have enough food to eat."

Out of his bleak circumstances came the beginnings of repentance. He accepted responsibility for his condition, saying, "I will get up and go to my father, and will say to him, 'Father, I have sinned against heaven, and in your sight; I am no longer worthy to be called your son; make me as one of your hired men'" (vv. 18-19). That was not a crafty ploy for free food, but a humble confession from his heart. He was genuinely sorry, not for his lack of money or food, but because of what he had done. In saying he had "sinned against heaven," he was acknowledging that he had sinned against God.

Humble and repentant, the younger son "got up and came to his father" (v. 20). Notice that Jesus didn't say the young man came to his village, farm, or home, but to his "father." He was emphasizing the relationship between the father and son.

While the younger son was still a long way off, "his father saw him and felt compassion for him, and ran and embraced him and kissed him. And the son said to him, 'Father, I have sinned against heaven and in your sight; I am no longer worthy to be called your son'" (vv. 20-21). But before he could say, "Make me as one of your day laborers," the father called for a celebration. That is what our heavenly Father is like. He is so anxious for us to come to Him that He embraces us with love and kisses even before all our words of confession can be uttered.

The father said to his servants, "Quickly bring out the best robe and put it on him, and put a ring on his hand and sandals on his feet; and bring the fattened calf, kill it, and let us eat and celebrate; for this son of mine was dead and has come to life again; he was lost and has been found" (vv. 22-24). In the spirit of forgiveness, the father provided his son with the best of everything he had. Similarly, God is a Father who loves all repentant sinners deeply. He embraces them, rejoices over them, and gives them His best.

THE FATHER'S RELATIONSHIP TO BELIEVERS

In John 5, Jesus speaks of the Father's intimate relationship with the Son, and the parable of the loving father in Luke 15 speaks of the Father's intimate relationship with believers. The same lessons Christ taught about the Father in John 5 are illustrated in that parable. The point is this: God's love for us is no less than His love for the Son. Let's see how that is so.

The Father Is One with His Children

In the parable, the younger son was prepared to tell his father, "I'm no longer worthy to be called your son." But when he arrived, his father ordered a celebration for "this son of mine" (v. 24). The Father, likewise, claims as His own the sinner who repents and comes to Him for forgiveness.

Christ emphasized our oneness with the Father when He said, "In My Father's house are many dwelling places; if it were not so, I would have told you; for I go to prepare a place for you" (John 14:2). Notice that there is only one house with many rooms. It is the Father's house. Heaven is not blocks of streets lined with many mansions. Our residence will not be found by going six blocks to the right and down a block. We all as believers will live in the Father's house because we are one with Him and members of the same family.

The Father Loves His Children

The father saw his younger son "while he was still a long way off" (Luke 15:20). Ever since his younger son went away, the father had apparently been watching for his return. Seeing his son in the distance, the father "felt compassion for him, and ran and embraced him and kissed him" (v. 20). Notice that the father was the one who took the initiative to love his son. The father didn't wait for his son to give a speech. He didn't say to himself, "I wonder what he's going to say when he gets here? How's he going to handle this?" We see that initiative also illustrated in the Parable of the Lost Sheep:

> *What man among you, if he has a hundred sheep and has lost one of them, does not leave the ninety-nine in the open pasture and go after the one which is lost until he finds it? And when he has found it, he lays it on his shoulders, rejoicing.*
> —LUKE 15:4-5

Every shepherd seeks a lost sheep, not merely as a matter of duty, but out of love. Like a shepherd seeking a lost lamb, the father was moved with pity and compassion in his innermost being. He ran to meet his son and fell on his neck with a passionate embrace, kissing him repeatedly and fervently.

Our heavenly Father loves us in the same way. Some believers, contrite and repentant over some sin they have committed, struggle to believe God loves and forgives them. But such doubt and fear have no biblical warrant, for our Father not only accepts us, but also runs to embrace us in love.

In the now-famous "Footprints," the story is told of a believer who died and went to heaven. The Father embraced him in love and said, "Son, I've been waiting for you." Together they looked back over how the man had lived his life. As they did so, the man noticed that sometimes there were two footprints in his life, and sometimes there were four. So he said, "Father, I understand the four footprints because that's when You walked with me. But why, Father, were there only two footprints at certain times?" The Father smiled and replied, "Those were the times I carried you."

That's how it is with God. He loves His children. He'll walk with them. And if He has to, He'll carry them.

The Father Blesses His Children

Abraham Lincoln was asked how he was going to treat the rebellious Southerners once they were defeated and returned to the Union of the United States. It is said that the President replied, "I will treat them as if they had never done anything wrong."

In the parable, that was how the father responded to his younger son, for he said to his servants, "Quickly bring out the best robe and put it on him" (Luke 15:22). Why the "best" robe? Because to the people of that day, that was a sign of belonging in the family.

You might think the son didn't deserve such a blessing. But that's not the point; it's the nature of the father that's the issue. If God gave us what we deserve, we'd be consumed. That's the wonder of God's love, isn't it? In spite of what we've done, He treats us like sons and daughters who have never done anything wrong.

The Father Gives Authority to His Children

The father ordered that a ring be put on his son's hand (v. 22). It was a signet ring, symbolizing family authority. When anything was done officially by a family, it was sealed and the signet ring of the family was impressed in the seal. If you had that ring, you could legally speak for the whole family.

Has the Father given authority to us as His children? Yes. Christ made that clear when He told His disciples, "You shall be My witnesses" (Acts 1:8). Paul said it this way: "We are ambassadors for Christ, as though God were making an appeal through us" (2 Cor. 5:20). We have the authority to act on God's behalf and tell others about Him. One day we will even have authority to judge the world and angels (1 Cor. 6:2-3)!

The Father Honors His Children

The father ordered his servants to put sandals on the feet of his son. Slaves went barefoot, but not free men. He wanted his son to be regarded with respect. The father also called for a celebration that included a feast, music, and dancing. He wanted everyone to join in honoring the son who, in a sense, had been dead but now was alive.

Our Father wants us to enjoy intimate fellowship with Him. Although we might occasionally stray from Him, He is always ready to receive us back and to give us more than we could ever desire or deserve. It's no wonder the apostle John said, "See how great a love the Father has bestowed on us, that we would be called children of God" (1 John 3:1).

What is God like? He is our loving Father. Is that how you think of Him?

11

THE GLORY OF OUR GOD

David Brainerd yearned for the salvation of Native Americans scattered along the colonial trails and farther west. From 1742 to 1747 he toiled among tribes in New York, New Jersey, and Pennsylvania. Initially he saw little to encourage him and seriously considered abandoning his labors among them altogether. But in time the situation reversed itself, and scores of Native Americans came to know Christ. Brainerd's poor health, however, eventually forced him to abandon his missionary efforts, and at age twenty-nine he died.

He spent his last days in the home of his celebrated friend Jonathan Edwards. Before his death, Brainerd consented to leave his diary with Edwards for publication. That volume has had an untold impact on the lives of others because it reveals Brainerd's devotion, earnestness, sincerity, and self-denying spirit. Missionaries such as Henry Martyn, William Carey, and Jim Elliot have spoken of the great inspiration they received from reading Brainerd's diary.

These are some of the last entries Brainerd made:

This day, I saw clearly that I should never be happy, yea, that God Himself could not make me happy, unless I could be in a capacity to "please and glorify Him forever." Take away this and admit me into all the fine havens that can be conceived of by men or angels, and I should still be miserable forever. . . .

Oh, to love and praise God more, to please Him forever! This my soul panted after and even now pants for while I write. Oh, that God might be glorified in the whole earth! . . .

Was still in a sweet and comfortable frame; and was again melted with desires that God might be glorified, and with longings to love and live to Him. . . . And oh, I longed to be with God, to behold His glory and to bow in His presence! (*The Life and Diary of David Brainerd,* edited by Jonathan Edwards [Grand Rapids, Mich.: Baker, 1989], pp. 357-367)

It is clear that Brainerd's desire was to magnify God's glory before the world. He also looked forward to his earthly departure because he longed to see the glory of God in heaven. What exactly does the phrase *the glory of God* refer to? It is the sum of who He is—the sum of His attributes and divine nature. Throughout history, God has endeavored to show all men and women His glory. Let's see how that is so.

GOD'S GLORY IN THE GARDEN

God's glory was present at the very beginning in the Garden of Eden. There He manifested Himself to Adam and Eve, who lived in His presence and enjoyed fellowship with Him. It's likely that God revealed His glory to them in some visible way. We see throughout Scripture that whenever God wanted to reveal Himself to certain people, He did so through a brilliant light called the *Shekinah*. That's a Hebrew word meaning "to dwell" or "to reside with." God revealed His glory to them so that they might recognize Him as the glorious God that He is and give Him the respect He is due.

Unfortunately, this manifestation of God's glory was only temporary. When Adam and Eve sinned, "They heard the sound of the LORD God walking in the garden in the cool of the day, and the man and his wife hid themselves from the presence of the LORD God among the trees of the garden" (Gen. 3:8). The

Fall broke their communion with Him, and they no longer delighted in His presence.

Furthermore, God expelled Adam and Eve from the Garden because they were no longer fit to be where His glory was. He even placed an angel with a sword at the entrance of the Garden to keep them out. The only way they could be restored to fellowship with God was by judgment. Ultimately, there is only one way for fallen humanity to enjoy fellowship with God, and that's through Jesus Christ, for He endured God's judgment on our behalf.

GOD'S GLORY ON MOUNT SINAI

God also revealed His glory to Moses. Although God commissioned him to lead Israel into the Promised Land, the thought of doing so intimidated him (Exod. 33:12-13).

The Lord responded, "My presence shall go with you, and I will give you rest" (v. 14). The Hebrew word translated "rest" refers not to a cessation of activity, but to protection and blessing. The Lord promised that He would be with Moses and would provide for the needs and safety of His people.

Show Me Your Glory!

Although the Lord's reply undoubtedly encouraged Moses, yet Moses wanted some kind of visible proof to verify that the Lord would indeed be with him. Therefore, he made this request: "I pray You, show me Your glory!" (v. 18). Moses was asking for an unveiled view of God!

The Lord replied, "I Myself will make all My goodness pass before you" (v. 19). That was a wonderful answer to Moses' prayer, for it was God's promise to put all His attributes on display before Moses. The Lord then explained how He would do that:

> I . . . will proclaim the name of the LORD before you; and I will be gracious to whom I will be gracious, and will show com-

*passion on whom I will show compassion. . . . [But] you can-
not see My face, for no man can see Me and live! . . . Behold,
there is a place by Me, and you shall stand there on the rock;
and it will come about, while My glory is passing by, that I will
put you in the cleft of the rock and cover you with My hand
until I have passed by. Then I will take My hand away and you
shall see My back, but My face shall not be seen.*

—vv. 19-23

The Lord was going to cover Moses with His hand as His
glory passed by. That way Moses would not see His face, which
is the essence of His Being. Scripture says that no man has ever
seen the Lord's face (John 1:18; 6:46; 1 John 4:12). If anyone
were to do so, he or she would be consumed. When the Lord
removed His hand, Moses would see the back of the Lord. What
does His back represent? The afterglow or radiance of the
Lord's glory. Of course, God does not actually have a face, hand,
or back. As we noted earlier, Scripture characterizes the Lord in
human terms to accommodate our finite understanding.

Perhaps God's afterglow is like the radiance of the sun. No
one has ever seen the actual sun. What we see are gaseous flames
that leap off the sun. If we were to stand close enough to see the
sun, we'd be consumed. Since the sun is that devastating and
brilliant, what must God be like? The glory of all creation is but
a partial and dim reflection of the Creator's full glory.

The Shining Face

The Lord then instructed Moses, saying:

*Come up in the morning to Mount Sinai, and present yourself
there to Me on the top of the mountain. No man is to come up
with you, nor let any man be seen anywhere on the mountain;
even the flocks and the herds may not graze in front of that
mountain.*

—EXOD. 34:2-3

When Moses reached the top of the mountain, "The LORD descended in the cloud and stood there with him as he called upon the name of the LORD" (v. 5).

In fulfillment of His earlier promise, the Lord passed by Moses, proclaiming, "The LORD, the LORD God, compassionate and gracious, slow to anger, and abounding in lovingkindness and truth; who keeps lovingkindness for thousands, who forgives iniquity, transgression and sin; yet He will by no means leave the guilty unpunished, visiting the iniquity of fathers on the children and on the grandchildren to the third and fourth generations" (vv. 6-7). That is God's composite characterization of His own glory.

Upon hearing those majestic words, Moses "made haste to bow low toward the earth and worship" (v. 8). For forty days God revealed His Law to Moses. When finally Moses came down from Mount Sinai, he "did not know that the skin of his face shone because of his speaking with Him [God]" (v. 29). His face was reflecting God's glory. When Aaron and the rest of Israel saw his shining face, they were afraid to come near him. Moses, however, called them to himself and spoke to them. Then he "put a veil over his face so that the sons of Israel would not look intently at the end of what was fading away" (2 Cor. 3:13). The glory didn't last.

That reminds me of a time when I went with my parents as a boy to an amusement park. In the park was a shop that sold objects that glow in the dark. I thought it was the greatest thing I'd ever seen. Since my parents said I could get one, I went inside. The lights were out, and everything was glowing. It was fantastic. I picked out something I really liked—something that glowed in different colors.

When I returned home, I waited until dark to take the figure out of the package. After unwrapping it, I set the figure on my dresser, but there was no glow. I thought, "We've been robbed!" My father, observing all this, said to me, "Do you know why your figure doesn't glow? It doesn't have any light of its own." My father held the figure up to a light for a minute or so and then handed it back to me. This time it glowed! But after an hour or so, it didn't glow anymore.

Similarly, Moses didn't have any glow or light of his own. Therefore, God chose to send him off that mountain with a little afterglow of His own glory.

GOD'S GLORY IN THE TABERNACLE

God also revealed His glory in the tabernacle (Exod. 40:34). The tabernacle included the holy of holies, which contained the ark of the covenant. On the top of the ark was the mercy seat, where the high priest sprinkled blood once a year as an atonement for the sins of the people.

It was on the mercy seat that the *Shekinah* of God dwelt or tabernacled, for God said to Moses, "There I will meet with you; and from above the mercy seat, from between the two cherubim which are upon the ark of the testimony, I will speak to you about all that I will give you in commandment for the sons of Israel" (25:22).

Another reminder to the people of God's glory was the encampment of Israel during the forty years of wandering. Whenever the people stopped to set up camp, the priests were to be the closest to the tabernacle. Just beyond the priests were the Levitic families, while the rest of the twelve tribes made up the outer ring. The tabernacle was located in the exact center of the tribes.

Why such an arrangement? It was to help the people focus on the glory of God in their midst. The glory would rise to the sky when He wanted them to move, and it would descend when He wanted them to camp.

GOD'S GLORY IN THE TEMPLE

After Solomon completed the temple, which was a permanent structure to replace the tabernacle, "The cloud filled the house of the LORD, so that the priests could not stand to minister because of the cloud, for the glory of the LORD filled the house of the LORD" (1 Kings 8:10-11). The temple was a magnificent edifice, unequaled in the world. From it God was again saying to the people, "See My glory. Focus on it. Recognize who I am, and give Me proper reverence and worship."

Although the temple was built to glorify God, the people did not honor Him as they should have. That was especially evident in the days of Ezekiel. In an amazing vision, that prophet details the pagan idolatry he witnessed taking place in the temple (Ezek. 8:2-17). The nation had gone rapidly downhill from the days of Solomon.

Because of the people's sin and their refusal to repent, God removed His glory from the temple. The departure was progressive but total. At first His glory departed briefly to the doorway of the temple, but then returned to its customary place at the mercy seat (Ezek. 9:3). It departed once again to the doorway, but this time it did not return (10:4). From the doorway it moved to the courtyard (v. 18). Borne on the wings of angels, God's glory then moved to the gate on the east side of the temple. Finally, it "went up from the midst of the city and stood over the mountain which is east of the city" (11:23). It was evident for all to see: God was abandoning His city because of its sin. Written over Israel was the word *Ichabod*, which means "the glory has departed."

GOD'S GLORY IN JESUS CHRIST

The Gospel of John begins: "In the beginning was the Word, and the Word was with God, and the Word was God. . . . And the Word became flesh, and dwelt among us, and *we saw His glory*, glory as of the only begotten from the Father, full of grace and truth" (1:1, 14, emphasis added).

But when Jesus Christ came into the world, His glory was veiled. He was among men, but most didn't know who He was.

Isaiah prophesied, "He had no beauty or majesty to attract us to him, nothing in his appearance that we should desire him" (53:2, NIV). Christ told His disciples, however, that in His Second Coming, "The Son of Man is going to come in the glory of His Father" (Matt. 16:27). That is, there will be a full display of His divine attributes. His blazing, unveiled glory will light up the whole universe.

Undoubtedly, Christ's promise for the future comforted the disciples; yet He knew they needed encouragement here and now as well. Therefore He said, "There are some of those who are standing here who will not taste death until they see the Son of Man coming in His kingdom" (v. 28). The Greek word translated "kingdom" here speaks of regal splendor and royal majesty. Three of the disciples were about to have a private showing of Christ's glory.

Six days later Jesus brought Peter, James, and John to a high mountain and "was transfigured before them; and His face shone like the sun, and His garments became as white as light" (Matt. 17:2). His form totally changed. The glory of God radiated from the inside out, the light within Him as brilliant as the sun.

Years later Peter testified, "We did not follow cleverly devised tales when we made known to you the power and coming of our Lord Jesus Christ, but we were eyewitnesses of His majesty" (2 Pet. 1:16). John was referring to the same thing when he said, "We saw His glory, glory as of the only begotten from the Father" (John 1:14). What did those disciples see? The blazing glory of God!

Presently the glory of God is displayed in Christ in the church. "To Him [God] be the glory in the church and in Christ Jesus to all generations forever and ever. Amen," said Paul (Eph. 3:21). The indwelling Christ is "the hope of glory" for every believer (Col. 1:27). God "has shone in our hearts to give the Light of the knowledge of the glory of God in the face of Christ. But we have this treasure in earthen vessels, so that the surpassing greatness of the power will be of God and not from our-selves" (2 Cor. 4:6-7).

Our purpose in life is not to live for ourselves, but to radiate God's glory. "Whether . . . you eat or drink or whatever you do, do all to the glory of God," said Paul (1 Cor. 10:31). That's a verse to live by. We are to have a passionate desire to do all we can to see that God receives the glory He deserves.

How will God reveal His glory in the future? As we noted earlier, there will be an unparalleled manifestation of His glory at the Second Coming. Our Lord Jesus Christ will come on the clouds of the sky "with power and great glory" (Matt. 24:30). His blazing glory will blind the world, and unbelievers will cry to the rocks and mountains, "Fall on us and hide us from the presence of Him who sits on the throne" (Rev. 6:16). Christ will destroy His enemies and receive the scepter of David's throne and so will reign in power and glory as King of kings and Lord of lords. Every tongue will "confess that Jesus Christ is Lord, to the glory of God the Father" (Phil. 2:11). King David spoke of Christ's glory this way:

> *Lift up your heads, O gates,*
> *And be lifted up, O ancient doors,*
> *That the King of glory may come in!*
> *Who is the King of glory?*
> *The* LORD *strong and mighty,*
> *The* LORD *mighty in battle.*
> *Lift up your heads, O gates,*
> *And lift them up, O ancient doors,*
> *That the King of glory may come in!*
> *Who is this King of glory?*
> *The* LORD *of hosts,*
> *He is the King of glory.*
>
> —Ps. 24:7-10

The final state of heaven will also be full of glory, for the New

Jerusalem "has no need of the sun or of the moon to shine on it, for the glory of God has illumined it, and its lamp is the Lamb" (Rev. 21:23). The brilliance of God lights the city. The apostle John, seeing a preview of that glory, proclaimed, "Amen, blessing and glory and wisdom and thanksgiving and honor and power and might, be to our God forever and ever. Amen" (Rev. 7:12). Are you willing to echo that "Amen" by living your life for God's glory?

12

THE WORSHIP OF
OUR GOD

Joachim Neander, a German hymn-writer, enriched the church
with this triumphant expression of worship:

> *Praise to the Lord, the Almighty,*
> *The King of creation!*
> *O my soul, praise Him,*
> *For He is thy health*
> *   and salvation!*
> *All ye who hear,*
> *Now to His temple draw near;*
> *Join me in glad adoration!*
>
> *Praise to the Lord!*
> *O let all that is in me adore Him!*
> *All that hath life and breath,*
> *Come now with praises*
> *   before Him.*
> *Let the Amen*
> *Sound from His people again:*
> *Gladly for aye we adore Him.*

Praise and adoration are integral aspects of worship. The
common New Testament word for worship, *proskuneo*, means
"to kiss" or "to reverence." It speaks of bowing before a supe-

rior with a sense of awe and homage. Christian worship is giving honor and respect to God. Let's see what Scripture says about how to do that.

WORSHIP OF THE GODHEAD

Christ pointed out that God the Father is to be the object of our worship when He said to the Samaritan woman, "True worshipers will worship the Father in spirit and truth" (John 4:23). God the Son is also to be worshiped. From the earliest years of the church, Christ was professed as Lord in baptism (Rom. 6:3-4), confessed as Lord in the church (Eph. 3:10-12), confessed as Lord in anticipation of the day when every knee will bow before Him (Phil. 2:9-11), and petitioned as Lord in time of need (Heb. 4:14-16). When Thomas saw the risen Christ, he worshiped Him, proclaiming, "My Lord and my God!" (John 20:28).

You might ask, "What about the Holy Spirit? Are we to worship Him as well?" Although there's nothing in Scripture that directly tells us to worship the Holy Spirit, He is, as we have seen, coequal with the other two Persons of the Trinity and is therefore worthy of our worship. All worship is energized in the power of the Spirit. It is the Spirit who allows us to come into God's presence and cry, "Abba! Father!" (Gal. 4:6; cf. Rom. 8:15). He is called both "the Spirit of God" (Matt. 3:16; Eph. 4:30) and "the Spirit of Christ" (Rom. 8:9; 1 Peter 1:11). We can worship the Spirit along with the Father and Son, but we must realize that the Spirit's unique ministry in the Church Age is to prompt us to worship the Son. The Son, in turn, calls us to worship the Father—even though all three are worthy of worship. This is true trinitarian worship: coming *to* the Father *through* the Son *in* the Spirit.

I'm concerned about people who vaguely worship God, who seem to worship only the Son, or who inordinately and incessantly focus only on the Holy Spirit. God is to be worshiped in His trinitarian fullness.

WORSHIP: THE GOAL OF SALVATION

Worship is the key to understanding the whole matter of salvation. That's because the goal of salvation is to produce true worshipers. They are the ones who "will worship the Father in spirit and truth; for such people the Father seeks to be His worshipers," said Jesus (John 4:23). When Paul evangelized the lost, even his persecutors said of him, "This man persuades men to worship God" (Acts 18:13). The heart and soul of evangelism is to call the lost to worship God. Not living a worshipful life is an affront to His holy nature and a rebellious act in His world.

The Gospel record is a chronicle of worship. When the wise men saw Christ at His birth, "they fell to the ground and worshiped Him" (Matt. 2:11). After the disciples witnessed Christ walking on the water and calming a storm, they worshiped Him, saying, "You are certainly God's Son!" (Matt. 14:33). A blind man whom Christ healed said, "We know that God does not hear sinners; but if anyone is God-fearing, and does His will, He hears him" (John 9:31). The man was pointing out that there are only two kinds of people: those God hears and those He doesn't. The contrast is between sinners and worshipers. To be a Christian is to be a worshiper.

In the Gospels we see that those who came to know Christ offered some kind of worshipful response—giving honor, homage, respect, reverence, adoration, and praise to God Himself. We are to do no less. The author of Hebrews said, "Since we are receiving a kingdom that cannot be shaken, let us be thankful, and so worship God acceptably with reverence and awe, for our 'God is a consuming fire'" (12:28-29, NIV; cf. Deut. 4:24). Acceptable worship is the result of salvation. Yet worship reaches its fullness when the believer willingly offers himself to God, worshiping Him with respect and godly fear.

CENTERING OUR THOUGHTS ON GOD

How can we cultivate a heart for worship? By centering our thoughts on God. Worship is an overflow of a mind renewed by the truth of God. We are to focus our whole mind on Him.

Centering our thoughts on God begins with what I like to call *discovery*. That is, when we discover a great truth about God, we begin to meditate on that truth until it captivates our whole thinking process. That in turn will lead to worship.

Sometimes it will not be a matter of discovering anything new. Perhaps we knew a truth but forgot it. Or maybe we still remember, but now we see it more clearly or from a different perspective.

If worship is based on meditation, and meditation is based on discovery, what is discovery based on? On time spent with God in prayer and the Word. It is sad that many view prayer primarily as a way to get things. We have lost sight of the companion aspect of prayer—of being still and aware of God's wonderful presence and just communing with Him there.

As believers, we are rooted and grounded in Christ, but how deep our roots grow and how beautiful our fruit appears will depend to a large degree on our process of discovery and meditation on God's wonderful truth. Where there is no discovery, there will be no meditation; where there is no meditation, there will be no worship.

When we try to focus on worship, we will find one major hindrance—self. Instead of allowing time for prayer, meditation, and worship, we are prone to fulfill our own desires. We tend to think about our own projects, activities, and needs, but not about God. One way to circumvent that tendency is to have a heart filled with discovery from our own study of God's Word. Even if we've learned it from someone else, we must meditate on spiritual truths and make them our own. By doing so, the Lord will fill our hearts with praise.

THE FRAGRANCE OF WORSHIP

In the Old Testament we find that God gave many instructions on how worship was to be carried out. Several of those instructions have great symbolic value and are vital teaching tools for us today. One of those visual aids, described by the Lord in the book of Exodus, is this:

> *Take for yourself spices, stacte and onycha and galbanum, spices with pure frankincense; there shall be an equal part of each. And with it you shall make incense, a perfume, the work of a perfumer, salted, pure, and holy. You shall beat some of it very fine, and put part of it before the testimony in the tent of meeting where I will meet with you; it shall be most holy to you. The incense which you shall make, you shall not make in the same proportions for yourselves; it shall be holy to you for the LORD. Whoever shall make any like it, to use as perfume, shall be cut off from his people.*
>
> —30:34-38

This perfume was probably the most lovely fragrance imaginable, but God said it would cost the people their lives if they made it for themselves. That's because the fragrance was holy, being designed only for God. When this incense rose to God, it was unique to Him. This pictures worship as a holy act that rises from a person's heart to God in heaven.

In the New Testament we read of another fragrant gift offered to God in worship. This time it was presented to God on earth—to the Lord Jesus Christ, God incarnate:

> *Jesus . . . came to Bethany where Lazarus was, whom Jesus had raised from the dead. So they made Him a supper there, and Martha was serving; but Lazarus was one of those reclining at the table with Him. Mary then took a pound of very costly perfume of pure nard, and anointed the feet of Jesus and wiped His feet with her hair; and the house was filled with the fragrance of the perfume.*
>
> —JOHN 12:1-3

Mary condescended to use that which was her glory—her hair (cf. 1 Cor. 11:15)—to wash the dusty, dirty feet of Jesus. And she didn't use water—she used a very expensive perfume. That is the essence of worship: It is self-effacing and lavish at its core.

Mary's sister, Martha, had a different focus. Mary made a habit of sitting at the feet of Christ, learning as much as she could from Him, while Martha wore herself to a frazzle serving. Christ previously had said that what Mary chose to do was better than all of Martha's serving (Luke 10:38-42).

Judas also had a different focus. When he saw what Mary did with the expensive ointment, he said, "Why was this perfume not sold for three hundred denarii [about a year's wages] and given to poor people?" (John 12:5). John explains that Judas said that "not because he was concerned about the poor, but because he was a thief, and as he had the money box, he used to pilfer what was put into it" (v. 6). Christ responded, "Let her alone. . . . For you always have the poor with you, but you do not always have Me" (vv. 7-8). Giving to those who are truly in need is important. But giving what we can to God when we have the opportunity to do so is infinitely more important than what we give to people—any people.

Mary's deed was an act of true worship. As the fragrance arose from her perfume, filling the room, it was a powerful symbol of a worshipful heart. That's what God is after.

We tend to be so pragmatic, don't we? We are a generation of Marthas—always busy. We have the church fine-tuned to a system, with all its programs and activities. And we are very careful not to waste our substance. Even what we give to God we tend to mark out very carefully, rather than pour out a year's wages and stoop humbly to wipe His feet with our hair.

I think a comparison of worship with service or ministry might help distinguish what true worship really is. To begin with, it is not the same as ministry. Ministry *comes down* to us from the Father, through the Son, in the power of the Holy Spirit, to one another in the form of spiritual gifts. Worship *goes up* from us, by the Spirit's power, through the Son, to the Father. Ministry *descends* from God to us, while worship *ascends* from us to God. Both must be in perfect balance. Unfortunately, we tend to be too ministry-oriented (like Martha) and not oriented enough toward worship. We need to learn from Mary how to sit at Jesus' feet and worship Him.

A wise minister wrote long ago:

> Come now, little man, put aside your business for a while, take refuge for a little from your tumultuous thoughts; cast off your cares, and let your burdensome distractions wait. Take some leisure for God; rest awhile in him. Enter into the chamber of your mind; put out everything except God and whatever helps you to seek him; close the door and seek him. Say now to God with all your heart: "I seek thy face, O Lord, thy face do I seek." (Cited by R. W. Southern in *Saint Anselm and His Biographer* [Cambridge: Cambridge University, 1963], p. 49)

A LAME OFFERING

Perhaps you're feeling motivated to worship God anew. I hope you do, but keep this one warning in mind: It is very easy to worship God with a wrong attitude. That's a sin the Israelites fell into. Because the priests were the leaders in this sin, the Lord rebuked them, saying:

> *"A son honors his father, and a servant his master. Then if I am a father, where is My honor? And if I am a master, where is My respect?" says the LORD of hosts to you, O priests who despise My name. But you say, "How have we despised Your name?" You are presenting defiled food upon My altar. But you say, "How have we defiled You?" In that you say, "The table [altar] of the LORD is to be despised."*
>
> —MAL. 1:6-7

The priests treated their worship with contempt. For them it became strictly routine. In fact, their sacrificing blind, sick, and lame animals on the Lord's altar was evidence of that. Because such animals were likely to die anyway, it was no loss for the priests to offer them to the Lord. Instead of offering the best animals, they offered the worst. That was a grievous sin, for the Mosaic Law made it clear that only flawless animals were to be sacrificed (Lev. 22:22-25).

The Lord continued His rebuke, saying:

> *"When you present the blind for sacrifice, is it not evil? And when you present the lame and sick, is it not evil? Why not offer it to your governor? Would he be pleased with you? Or would he receive you kindly? . . . Oh that there were one among you who would shut the gates, that you might not uselessly kindle fire on My altar! I am not pleased with you . . . nor will I accept an offering from you. For from the rising of the sun even to its setting, My name will be great among the nations, and in every place incense is going to be offered to My name, and a grain offering that is pure; for My name will be great among the nations."*
>
> —MAL. 1:8, 10-11

The Lord was saying, "If this is how you treat Me, how do you think I'm going to treat you?" There are some things God simply will not accept, and one of them is worship offered in a materialistic, self-styled, halfhearted way.

The Israelites came to regard the sacrificial system with contempt. To them the whole exercise of worship was just a big pain in the neck. They probably said something like, "What a drag! We have to go to the temple and worship again. Let's just get it over with by getting rid of some lame or blind animals—we don't need them anyway!" But as Charles L. Feinberg pointed out:

> How could God accept such a sham and insult as satisfactory to Him? And it was not because of poverty, but the difficulty was greed. The curse is pronounced upon the deceiver who

thinks he can vow—in such cases the best was promised to God—a proper sacrifice, and then fulfill the vow with an unsuitable animal. Such offerings were an insult to the majesty of God, for He is a great King. (*The Minor Prophets* [Chicago: Moody Press, 1951], p. 254)

The people were merely going through the motions of offering a sacrifice instead of coming before the Lord with a humble heart and a desire to honor Him. They showed further contempt by bad-mouthing God, as evidenced by this reprimand:

> *"Your words have been arrogant against Me," says the* LORD. *"Yet you say, 'What have we spoken against You?' You have said, 'It is vain to serve God; and what profit is it that we have kept His charge, and that we have walked in mourning before the* LORD *of hosts?'"*
>
> —MAL. 3:13-14

They had decided they didn't make enough money serving the Lord—there wasn't enough profit in it!

What can we learn from that wrong example? The importance of worshiping God with the right attitude. To move ourselves along that path, we must think through questions like these: *Is God at the center of my life? Does He dominate my thinking? Am I perpetually grateful to Him for all He has done for me? Have I become distracted from God-centered living because of pride, greed, selfishness, or materialism?*

It is not the sacrifice itself that God is after, but the attitude of thanksgiving behind it. That's why God said:

> *"Every beast of the forest is Mine,*
> *The cattle on a thousand hills.*
> *I know every bird of the mountains,*
> *And everything that moves in the field is Mine.*
> *If I were hungry, I would not tell you,*
> *For the world is Mine, and all it contains.*

> *Shall I eat the flesh of bulls*
> *Or drink the blood of male goats?*
> *Offer to God a sacrifice of thanksgiving*
> *And pay your vows to the Most High;*
> *And call upon Me in the day of trouble;*
> *I shall rescue you, and you will honor Me. . . .*
> *Now consider this, you who forget God . . .*
> *He who offers a sacrifice of thanksgiving honors Me;*
> *And to him who orders his way aright*
> *I shall show the salvation of God."*
>
> —PS. 50:10-15, 22-23

DRAWING NEAR TO GOD

How can we prepare ourselves to worship God in an acceptable way? The author of Hebrews tells us:

> *Let us draw near with a sincere heart in full assurance of faith, having our hearts sprinkled clean from an evil conscience and our bodies washed with pure water.*
>
> —10:22

The phrase "let us draw near" is a call to worship. Acceptable worship does not happen spontaneously. Preparation is essential. For those who would heed that call, there are four checkpoints to consider.

The Checkpoint of Sincerity

We are to draw near "with a sincere heart." Our heart is to be devoted to glorifying God. It is hypocritical to be worshiping God when we really are apathetic or preoccupied with self. God wants us to worship Him with our whole heart.

The Checkpoint of Fidelity

We are to draw near "in full assurance of faith." The Hebrews were clinging to Old Covenant forms of worship, but the New

Covenant made it clear there were to be no more ceremonies or sacrifices. Each person had to be willing to say, "I'm coming to God in full confidence that I am no longer under a system of ceremony. I come fully by faith in Jesus Christ." We are to be fully assured that God accepts our worship because of our faith in Christ.

The Checkpoint of Humility

We are to draw near to God "having our hearts sprinkled clean from an evil conscience." That is, we are to come to God with the knowledge that we're unworthy to be in His presence. The only reason we can come to Him is because of the blood of Christ, which was shed on the cross to cleanse us from our sin.

The Checkpoint of Purity

Before we approach God, we're to have "our bodies washed with pure water." That refers to a daily cleansing. Before we can worship, we have to deal with any known sins in our lives through confession (1 John 1:9). Even though our hearts were cleansed at the cross, our feet still pick up the dust of the world from day to day.

Every time we worship, we must prepare ourselves by asking questions like these: *Am I being sincere? Is my heart fixed on God, and is it undivided? Am I seeing Him anew in the Word through discovery and meditation so I am compelled to draw near to Him? Am I fully assured that my simple faith in Christ brings me before God's throne? Am I coming humbly, realizing I can draw near only because of what Christ has done for me? Is there any sin in my life I haven't dealt with?*

Perhaps you have been attending church for years, but you've never really drawn near to God, nor have you sensed His nearness—even in your own private devotions and prayers. Now you know, or perhaps have been reminded, that God has redeemed you so that you might worship Him. That is the purpose for which you were created. Know also and be encouraged that in contemplating the character of God—as you have throughout this book—you have placed yourself in a position for God's Word to produce the spirit of true worship in your heart. Continue living in the light of God's attributes as revealed in His Word, and ask that you might know more and more by experience what it is to worship Him in spirit and truth. That is a prayer our great God will delight in answering.

STUDY GUIDE

CHAPTER 1:
OUR TRIUNE GOD

Summarizing the Chapter

God exists in three distinct Persons; yet any attempt to conclusively prove His existence falls short. His existence must be accepted by faith.

GETTING STARTED (CHOOSE ONE)

1. Your assignment is to prove the existence of God. What methods can you use to gather your evidence? What do you suppose will be your most reliable source?
2. Think of some earthly illustrations of the Trinity, other than eggs or water. In what ways does the illustration fail to characterize the Trinity?

ANSWERING THE QUESTIONS

1. What three reasons did Freud give to support his theory that man needs to invent a God for himself? Explain each one.
2. Compare Freud's view of religion to other ideas about God that you have seen or heard.
3. Why does the scientific method fall short in being able to prove the existence of God?
4. Ultimately, how does a Christian acknowledge the existence of God?
5. Explain how God can be both a personal and a spiritual being.
6. What does the fact that there is only one God mean with respect to salvation?
7. In what important events in the New Testament do we see obvious evidence of the work of the Trinity?
8. According to J. I. Packer, what can happen to our understanding of the Trinity when we attempt to explain it?

FOCUSING ON PRAYER

Thank God for how He has revealed Himself to all mankind both in His Word and in creation. Thank Him for revealing Himself to you personally and for giving you the faith to believe in Him. And thank Him for being a trustworthy God, because He is the only God.

APPLYING THE TRUTH

Read Deuteronomy 6:4-5 and Mark 12:29-30. How can you tell if this command of God, central to both the Old and New Testaments, is really the priority of your life? If it is not your priority, what is? In Deuteronomy 6:6-9 God provided some specific ways that the Israelites could make the command their priority. In what specific ways can you make those verses a reality in your spiritual life?

CHAPTER 2:
OUR FAITHFUL, UNCHANGING GOD

Summarizing the Chapter

God's faithfulness to His children is proven by His promise to Abraham. We can trust in His faithfulness because it is based on His unchanging character.

GETTING STARTED (CHOOSE ONE)

1. Suppose you received a letter in the mail from a close, trustworthy friend. In it he or she asks you to leave your home, relatives, and friends and, with only your immediate family, move to a different part of the country. The letter doesn't tell you why or what you will find when you get there. Would you go? Why or why not?

2. We all make plans for various things at our work or home or for our own enjoyment. How often do your plans end up getting changed? What kinds of things alter your plans?

ANSWERING THE QUESTIONS

1. What did Abraham know about the journey God asked him to take? Why did he go?

2. How could Abraham willingly give his son Isaac as an offering to God even though he knew that God's promises to him must be fulfilled in Isaac?

3. Why did God choose Abraham to be the progenitor of the nation Israel?

4. Why did God make His covenant with Abraham completely dependent on Himself alone as the keeper of it?

5. Explain how Abraham is the spiritual father of all who believe in God. If believers are true sons of Abraham, how secure can they be? Why?

6. Why did God guarantee His promise to Abraham with an oath (Heb. 6:13-18)?

7. Explain how Christ has secured us through being the anchor of our soul and having entered within the veil (Heb. 6:19-20).

8. Mention a couple of biblical passages that seem to imply changes in God, and discuss their meanings.

9. What does God's unchanging character mean to believers? Explain.

FOCUSING ON PRAYER

Thank God for choosing you for salvation. Thank Him that your salvation did not depend on anything you did or ever could do. Finally, thank Him for Christ's ongoing intercession on your behalf.

APPLYING THE TRUTH

Reread Genesis 22:1-14. Put yourself in Abraham's shoes. How would you have responded when God first told Abraham what He wanted him to do? Now think of something you have sensed that God has wanted you to do recently, such as showing love to an individual you can hardly stand, or changing your spending habits and becoming a better steward of what He has given you. Based on Abraham's example, what are the benefits of being obedient to God? Keeping that in mind, what are *you* going to do and when?

CHAPTER 3:
OUR HOLY GOD

Summarizing the Chapter

God is holy, and His holiness is the standard that everyone who claims to be a Christian should desire.

GETTING STARTED (CHOOSE ONE)

1. When you contrast your sinfulness with God's holiness, what kinds of thoughts come to mind?
2. If you are a parent, you have established certain rules of conduct and specific duties that your children must perform. How do you feel when your children are disobedient? How does that affect your love for them?

ANSWERING THE QUESTIONS

1. What does it mean to be holy? How can people become holy?
2. Explain why God, while hating sin, willingly redeems a repentant sinner.
3. In what ways is God's holiness expressed for all to see? What is the greatest expression of His holiness?
4. After King Uzziah's death, how did the people respond to Isaiah's call to repent of their sin?
5. What reassurance did God give Isaiah concerning the loss of Uzziah?
6. Describe the seraphim. What do certain features of their appearance indicate about God's holiness?
7. What happened to Isaiah as a result of being in God's holy presence? What do believers miss when they don't understand the holiness of God?
8. Why is it important for Christians to live holy lives?

FOCUSING ON PRAYER

Follow David's lead by asking God to reveal to you the sin in your heart (Ps. 139:23-24). Then ask Him to create a clean heart within you—one that wants only to obey and love Him.

APPLYING THE TRUTH

Read Romans 7:7-25. List the statements Paul made that you can particularly identify with. As a Christian, the conflict of delighting in God's will but failing to carry it out perfectly should be present in your life. Even though you know that Christians sin, you must resist the temptation to rationalize what you do wrong. Sin brings nothing but guilt, misery, and despair to the person who refuses to deal with it. Follow the lead of the psalmist who said, "Your word I have treasured in my heart, that I may not sin against You" (Ps. 119:11).

CHAPTER 4:
OUR OMNISCIENT GOD

Summarizing the Chapter

Since God knows everything, He knows every detail of our lives. He has perfect knowledge and wisdom.

GETTING STARTED (CHOOSE ONE)

1. How many things about yourself don't you know physically (e.g., how many hairs are on your head)? What don't you know about yourself spiritually?
2. What are some specific ways that people attempt to hide their unrighteousness? Which of those have you been guilty of?

ANSWERING THE QUESTIONS

1. Explain what God's knowledge is like. Is there anything about us that He doesn't know?
2. Why can people who hide their sin be described as being behind false religious fronts like whitewashed tombs?
3. What kind of perspective ought we to have when it appears as if the ungodly prosper in their wickedness?
4. Why is human wisdom defective in dealing with anything of a spiritual nature?
5. Describe the effect of God's multicolored wisdom in His plan of salvation.
6. In what ways did Christ's omniscience prove beneficial to Peter?
7. How can God's omniscience provide comfort to those who are His children?

FOCUSING ON PRAYER

Read Psalm 147:7-19 and make that your prayer of thankfulness to God for what He has done for you.

APPLYING THE TRUTH

Read 1 Corinthians 1:18-31. Think about how people today regard God's wisdom as foolish. Now look at your own life. Are there any ways in which you adhere to the wisdom of the world? What does James 3:13-18 say about the wisdom of the world? What does that passage say about the wisdom of God? What aspects of your life do you need to bring under the authority of God's wisdom?

CHAPTER 5:
OUR OMNIPRESENT GOD

Summarizing the Chapter

God is with His children wherever they are. Their worship of Him, therefore, is never limited to any time or place.

GETTING STARTED (CHOOSE ONE)

1. Has there been a time in your life when you faced great danger or thought that your life or health might be threatened in some way? How did you handle your fear?
2. Can you think of any modern illustrations that might capture an aspect of God's omnipresence? Think of a substance that fills a container, or something that is not limited by time or by place.

ANSWERING THE QUESTIONS

1. What are the various representations of God in the world—past, present, and future?
2. Can God become impure by His contact with impure things? Why or why not?
3. Since God is spirit and He cannot be confined to any one place, how does that affect our worship of Him?
4. What was Jesus foretelling when He said, "An hour is coming, and now is, when the true worshipers will worship the Father in spirit and truth" (John 4:23)?
5. Explain how God's abiding presence can bring comfort to believers who are hurting.
6. How should God's abiding presence in our lives motivate us with regard to our sin?
7. How does Habakkuk's story provide a clear example of Paul's command to be anxious for nothing?
8. What principle did Habakkuk learn from his experience?

FOCUSING ON PRAYER

Philippians 4:5-6 says, "The Lord is near. Be anxious for nothing." Lay before God right now any anxiety you have in your heart. Ask Him to replace it with the assurance that He is with you and that He will never leave you or forsake you.

APPLYING THE TRUTH

Each day this week, the moment you wake up, begin the day by acknowledging God. Think ahead the night before of something specific you want to thank Him for, or an attribute of His to praise Him for. Consider making this a lifetime practice.

CHAPTER 6:
OUR OMNIPOTENT GOD

Summarizing the Chapter

God is omnipotent, which means He has the ability and power to do anything. *His* power is the source of our spiritual power.

GETTING STARTED (CHOOSE ONE)

1. Name some people or things that exhibit great power. Who or which do you believe is the most powerful? Now try to imagine something even more powerful than that. Even then you haven't come close to God's awesome power.
2. Reflect on a few of the trials you've had to endure in your life. How did you handle them? In what ways do you suppose God's power was active in helping you endure?

ANSWERING THE QUESTIONS

1. What does God's omnipotence allow Him to do? Explain.
2. In what ways is God's power expressed in creation? What would happen if He were to relinquish His sustaining power?
3. How does God express His power in your salvation?
4. Why was Jesus able to confess openly the truth about His lordship, messianic identity, and sovereign authority?
5. In what four ways is God's power the source of our spiritual power?
6. What did Old Testament believers know about God's ability to raise the dead?
7. What is the only proper response to God's power?

FOCUSING ON PRAYER

Thank God for how He has exhibited His power in creation, salvation, and resurrection. Praise Him especially for your salvation. Thank Him that through His power He will complete the work He began in you and will bring you to complete maturity.

APPLYING THE TRUTH

Read Philippians 1:6. We know that God completes what He starts because He has the power to do so. How does that truth relate to your salvation and your consequent growth in Him? How does that also relate to your relationship with other believers, especially your concerns about their spiritual growth? Even though things may not be progressing as you would want, what must you trust in?

CHAPTER 7:
THE WRATH OF OUR GOD

Summarizing the Chapter

God is a wrathful God because He hates sin. It is vital that we understand and appreciate this attribute or we will not fully comprehend God's love.

GETTING STARTED (CHOOSE ONE)

1. What happens when you get angry about something? What do you do? What do you feel? And what do you think about your anger? How often would you attribute your anger to your own sinfulness?
2. What are some ways God's wrath is being revealed today? On the other hand, name some things going on in the world you are surprised God hasn't judged yet.

ANSWERING THE QUESTIONS

1. Describe some of what Scripture says about God's wrath.
2. What is one great benefit of understanding how much God hates sin?
3. Explain how God's wrath is different from human anger.
4. In what events has God already revealed His wrath?
5. How do certain Hebrew and Greek terms describe God's holy reaction to sin?
6. According to Romans 1:18, against what does God unleash His wrath? Explain.
7. What is the worst crime ever committed in the universe? What is the penalty?
8. What did Nebuchadnezzar believe about himself? How did God alter his perspective?

FOCUSING ON PRAYER

Pray for those you know who are "without hope and without God in the world" (Eph. 2:12, NIV). Ask the Lord to give you a greater sensitivity to ways to approach them and to help you know what to tell them. Ask Him to make you bold in communicating the wrath that is headed their way (cf. Eph. 6:19).

APPLYING THE TRUTH

Make a list of unbelievers whom God has especially put on your heart. Begin strategizing about the best way to share the Gospel with them. Remember, while you must communicate the facts of the Gospel, the ways you do so will be different for each person.

CHAPTER 8:
THE GOODNESS OF OUR GOD

Summarizing the Chapter

God is good, extending love, mercy, and grace to all who are caught in the clutches of sin. God's goodness brings about repentance, causing us to long for Him and to be thankful for all that He does.

GETTING STARTED (CHOOSE ONE)

1. In what specific ways are you blessed by God? How many of those blessings do you automatically take for granted? Which ones would you be unable to live without?
2. What kinds of things can break the bond of love between individuals? Give some examples of times when you have personally experienced or witnessed such a break.

ANSWERING THE QUESTIONS

1. Give a definition of God's goodness.
2. Explain how every individual personally experiences the goodness of God.
3. Why is God patient in holding back His judgment on sinful mankind?
4. What is the supreme expression of God's goodness?
5. Describe what Christ endured in His scourging and crucifixion.
6. Why did God allow His Son to die on the cross?
7. How did Paul answer the question, What can make Christ stop loving you? Explain.

FOCUSING ON PRAYER

Thank God right now for sending Christ to die in your place, paying the penalty that all your sin deserves. Thank Christ for being your Mediator in heaven, where He sits at God's right hand making continual intercession for you. Finally, thank God for guaranteeing the final outcome of your salvation—your final glorification in heaven.

APPLYING THE TRUTH

Read Isaiah 53. Which verses describe the types of sacrifices Christ made for us? Which show what His supreme sacrifice accomplished for sinners? In your own words, describe what this reveals about God's goodness to His people.

CHAPTER 9:
OUR SOVEREIGN GOD

Summarizing the Chapter

God is sovereign—He does as He pleases. No person or circumstance can defeat His counsel or thwart His purposes.

GETTING STARTED (CHOOSE ONE)

1. Relate the circumstances of your conversion to Jesus Christ. In what ways do you see God's sovereignty at work in leading you to commit your life to Him?
2. What events or circumstances in your life that you consider bad has God actually used for your good? Describe the beneficial results in each instance.

ANSWERING THE QUESTIONS

1. Define what it means to say that God is sovereign.
2. What are three theological senses in which God elects people? Describe each.
3. When and why did God choose certain people for salvation?
4. What good things does God use for our spiritual benefit?
5. How does God use suffering in our lives to work for our good?
6. How can temptation work out for our spiritual benefit?
7. How can God use sin and all its wickedness for our ultimate good?

FOCUSING ON PRAYER

Thank God for His consistent, unchanging devotion to working out your life for your ultimate benefit. Thank Him for every day in which He continually molds you to become more and more like Christ. Ask Him to help you be more sensitive to His leading each day.

APPLYING THE TRUTH

For the next week make a list of events, circumstances, or trials you encounter over which you have no control. Each day refer to your list to see how that event may be shaping you, either physically, mentally, or spiritually. Be sure to honor God as you see those things working out for your good.

CHAPTER 10:
OUR FATHER GOD

Summarizing the Chapter

More than any other concept of God, Jesus emphasized God's role as His Father. And just as Jesus has an intimate relationship with God the Father, so do all who have been adopted into His family.

Getting Started (Choose One)

1. Describe your most intimate human relationship. What is characteristic about that relationship that is not true of any other relationship you have?
2. In what ways do you see God as your heavenly Father? What characteristics of your relationship with your earthly father do you find in your relationship with God? What aspects are exclusive to your relationship with God?

Answering the Questions

1. Who knows God better than anyone else? Why?
2. Explain the clear case Scripture makes that God and Christ are one.
3. What was the joy that motivated Christ to endure the cross? Be specific.
4. What is the significance of the believer's adoption into the family of God?
5. What eventually convinced the prodigal son of his need to return to his father's house?
6. What characteristics of God do you see represented by the father of the prodigal son?
7. In what ways is God's love for us no less than it is for His Son?

Focusing on Prayer

Read Psalm 139:23-24, and ask God to reveal to you the hidden sins of your heart. As He answers that prayer, have no fear as you go to Him and repent of whatever He shows you. Ask Him to help you stiffen your resolve against the sins to which you are most susceptible.

Applying the Truth

Review the Parable of the Prodigal Son. What can you learn about repentance from that parable? Is there anything that should prevent you from repenting of your sin? How will your heavenly Father receive you when you face Him with a repentant heart? Remember this parable when you are tempted to not deal with your sin because you fear how God will deal with you.

Chapter 11:
The Glory of Our God

Summarizing the Chapter

The glory of God is simply the sum of who He is—the sum of His attributes and divine nature.

Getting Started (Choose One)

1. As a Christian, what can you do to glorify God? How many of those things are you doing consistently?
2. Describe an eyewitness. Why are you likely to believe an eyewitness?

ANSWERING THE QUESTIONS

1. Why was God's visible manifestation to Adam and Eve only temporary?
2. How did God grant Moses' request to see His glory?
3. What happened to Moses' face after seeing God's glory? Was that a permanent condition? Explain.
4. Why did God want the Israelites to keep the tabernacle in the center of their camp?
5. Explain the term *Ichabod* and what it meant for the nation of Israel.
6. Why didn't people see God's glory as Jesus walked this earth? Why did Jesus give a few of His disciples an opportunity to see His glory?
7. Where is God's glory presently on display? Explain.
8. How will God reveal His glory in the future?

FOCUSING ON PRAYER

Thank God for the opportunity He has given you to glorify Him. Ask God to show you some specific ways you can glorify Him by your actions. Thank Him also for the glory you will experience when you go to be with Christ in heaven.

APPLYING THE TRUTH

As a constant reminder of what your duty to God is, memorize Psalm 100, a short psalm that exhorts us to praise God for all He has done for us.

CHAPTER 12:
THE WORSHIP OF OUR GOD

Summarizing the Chapter

The worship of God and His Son, Jesus Christ, is central to the life of the Christian. The goal of salvation is to produce true worshipers, and we fulfill that role when we worship God in spirit and in truth.

GETTING STARTED (CHOOSE ONE)

1. When you want to get to know someone better, what do you need to do? More specifically, what does the person need to see about how you regard him or her? How does that apply to God?
2. What types of ministry are you involved in at your church? How much time does it consume? How much time do you spend on leisure activities—things that, if you were to really analyze them, have no spiritual value?

ANSWERING THE QUESTIONS

1. Define Christian worship.
2. Who is the object of our worship? Explain.
3. What is the main reason God redeems people?

4. How can you begin to center your thoughts on God? What must you do to cultivate that kind of thinking?
5. How does Mary's act of washing the feet of Jesus with her hair and with expensive perfume symbolize worship?
6. Contrast worship with ministry.
7. How did the priests of Malachi's day dishonor God through their religious practices?
8. What should you do to prepare to worship God?

FOCUSING ON PRAYER

The only way we can truly worship God is to be sure that our motives are right and that there is no unconfessed sin in our lives. Bow before God right now and ask Him to reveal the true motives of your heart. If you have wrong motives, or if there is any sin you have been holding on to, confess it all to God right now. Ask Him to help you to be sincerely repentant of those things, which means being willing never to do them again.

APPLYING THE TRUTH

The goal of this book has been to bring you closer to God, so that your worship of Him might be true and right for all the right reasons. Make a copy of the four-point checklist at the end of this chapter. Keep it in your Bible. Before you spend time with God, review that checklist until sincerity, fidelity, humility, and purity become the automatic motivations of your heart.

SCRIPTURE INDEX

GENERAL INDEX